# CONTENTS

*Introduction*     v

1. What is the Lean Methodology?     1
2. What is Six Sigma?     19
3. Are There Different Levels to Implementing Six Sigma?     40
4. What Tools Can We Use?     49
5. The Steps of Lean Six Sigma     60
6. Figuring Out the Scope of Your Project     66
7. Who is Responsible?     73
8. How to Know What Solution is the Best?     76
9. Common Issues That Can Show Up in Lean Six Sigma     82
10. The Certification Levels of Six Sigma     90
11. Tips to Make Six Sigma Work for You     100

*Afterword*     109

# INTRODUCTION

Congratulations on purchasing *Lean Six Sigma* and thank you for doing so.

The following chapters will discuss all the things that you and your business need to know if you would like to take some of the ideas of Lean Six Sigma and implement them into your business in no time. This is a great methodology that helps you to take some of the processes that you are using today, and makes them better. It helps to reduce the amount of risks that you take, can cut down on the wastes that are costing you money, can provide a superior customer service experience, and a better product, to your customers and can give you higher revenues in the process. There is so much to enjoy about Six Sigma, especially when we add Lean to it, and this guidebook will take some time to explore this.

To start this guidebook, we are going to spend some time looking more at what the Lean methodology is all about. This is a methodology that is really successful and can help drive your business to the next level in no time if you learn how to work with it well. We can then move on to Six Sigma and some of the things that you need to know about that methodology as well, including the different methods that go with it and some of the benefits. It won't take long to see how great these two processes are going to work with one another.

From there, we are going to look a bit more at Six Sigma and how we can use this well. we will first start to look at the different levels, or the different roles, that come with implementing this process in your own business. And then we can explore some of the tools that work well with this process, including the 5 Why's and some of the analyses that we can work on. Then we need to move on to how we can follow all the steps that are necessary to work with lean Six Sigma, and what those steps entail.

Once we are done with some of that, it is time to look at the practical uses of Six Sigma and how we can go about these projects. We will explore how to pick a project and the project scope that we want to work with, who is responsible for each leg of the journey with Six Sigma, and how to know which solution out of all the options that come up will solve your problems and actually be the best one to use.

This leaves us to some of the final thoughts that we need to explore when it comes to Lean Six Sigma. We are going to look at a few of the most common issues that these kinds of projects can face and how to deal with them, what the various levels of certification in lean Six Sigma are all about and which level you may be the most interested in and more. Then we can end this guidebook with a look at some of the best tips that will ensure you can take Lean Six Sigma and make it work really well in your own business.

There are so many benefits to working with Lean Six Sigma and seeing some of the great things that it is able to do for your business. It can eliminate the waste, no matter which form it shows up as in your business. When you are ready to learn a bit more about what Lean Six Sigma is all about and how this process works, and what we are able to do with it to improve customer satisfaction while increasing or own profits in the process then make sure to check out this guidebook to get started.

There are plenty of books on this subject on the market, thanks again for choosing this one! Every effort was made to ensure it is full of as much useful information as possible; please enjoy it!

# WHAT IS THE LEAN METHODOLOGY?

THE FIRST PART of the equation that we need to spend some time on here is the Lean methodology. Six Sigma and Lean work well together, but to really see some of the benefits and what they can do together to help our business, it is important to get a closer look at how this will work on its own. So we are going to take some time to learn a bit more about the Lean Methodology and what it is all about.

What is Lean?

The core idea that comes with the Lean methodology is that we need to maximize the value that we can provide to the customer while minimizing the amount of waste that we create in the process. To make it easier to work with, being Lean means that we are going to create some more value for customers without using as many resources to do it, especially the resources that are not necessary to get the work done.

. . .

*A*n organization that is Lean understands that value to the customer and it is going to focus some of its key processes on increasing this as much as possible. The ultimate goal here is to provide the perfect amount of value to the customer through a perfect value creation process. It is hopeful that we are able to get our waste down to zero, though as low as possible will be beneficial in this process as well.

*T*o accomplish all of this, the thinking that goes with Lean is going to change p the focus of your management from optimizing the assets, technologies and vertical departments on their own to optimizing the flow of products and services through the whole value stream, going in a way that is more horizontal so that the product and service can get through the whole process and reach the customer as soon as possible.

*E*liminating waste along entire streams of vale, rather than at a few isolated points, is going to create a process that is not going to require as much effort from your employees, less capital, less space, and even less time to make the products and the services. You can also work on this process to get it done with fewer costs and fewer defects compared to some of the traditional systems that you may have used in business.

*W*ith this method, when it is used well, companies are then able to respond to some of the changing desires of the customer with a lot of variety, with quality that is still high, lower costs, and throughput times that are very fast. You will also find that through this process, the idea of information management is a lot easier and more accurate as well.

When we are able to cut down the waste while increasing the amount of value that we can provide to our customers, it is always going to be a good thing. This can often be the little part that will boost us up above the competition and will ensure that we get our customers to come back again and again. And the best part is that we will be able to do so while increasing or own profits in the process.

## Lean Can Work with Everything

One of the biggest misconceptions that come with this is that Lean is something that we are able to use only for manufacturing. This is not true. Lean is able to work with all types of businesses and every process that you can think about. It is not really a cost reduction program or a tactic program, but a way of thinking and acting for the company as a whole and this can make it really useful overall for everyone to improve what they are doing.

You will find that businesses in all services and industries, including even governments and healthcare, are able to use some of the principles of Lean as a way that they can think and do things. This makes them more efficient with what they do. There are other companies who may not use the term lean, but they will label it something else and use it in their own system. This helps to make it fit better with their needs, but it still follows a lot of the principles that we are able to see with Lean.

. . .

$\mathcal{T}$he term lean is something that was originally coined to describe the business that Toyota was using during the late 1980s. this was so successful for the company to ensure that they could still go through and provide a really high-quality system to their customers, while keeping costs down and ensuring that they would not miss out on the important things.

## $\mathcal{M}$ore About Lean

The best way to think about Lean and what we are able to do with it is to remember that it provides us with a group of tools that we can bring up to help us figure out whether there is some waste in some of our processes or our current systems. Lean is all about finding and then reducing the amount of waste that is in the system and helping us to be more efficient. There are a few businesses that are going to look at the Lean processes because they are looking to reduce and fix some of the wastes and the issues that show up, and that can save them a lot of money while improving employee morale and helping them to make their customers happier.

$\mathcal{W}$ith lean, there is also a bigger focus on finding ways to reduce costs, while at the same time being able to improve how production goes any time that is a possibility. This is something that we can accomplish by identifying the small steps that we need to work on, and then figuring out what we can do to improve our processes from there. The steps do not have to be big or complicated, but they will make some of the changes that we need. Some of the tools that we are able to use, and the steps that we can follow, to get the most out of this methodology include:

1. Pull systems
2. Single minute exchange of die, or the SMED.
3. Single point of scheduling
4. Mixed model processing
5. Total productive maintenance
6. Multi-process handling
7. Rank order clustering
8. Control charts
9. A restructuring process with the working cells
10. The elimination of a process called time batching
11. Error proofing
12. 5 S value stream mapping.

*B*eyond the tools above, Lean is going to be made up of a few principles, which are all loosely connected thanks to the idea of reduction of costs and eliminating wastes as much as possible. These would include load leveling, continuous improvement, production flow, visual control, automation, flexibility, waste minimization, building up some good relationships with the suppliers, pull processing and reliable quality and more.

*W*hen these principles are used in the proper manner, they are going to result in a bit increase in the amount of profitability. When it is used in the proper way and it is given the opportunity, this kind of process is going to strive in order to make sure that all necessary items get the space they need during the right periods of time. But most importantly, is that it is going to work to make sure that the ideal amount of items will move as needed so that your workflow remains stable, while still allowing for any alterations that are needed without all the waste.

*T*his is often seen as something that Lean is able to accomplish thanks to all of the great tools that come with it, but there is an issue that we need to address. For this process to work, you need to get everyone in the company to agree to use it and to go along with the new process. You can be all into it on your own, but if there are a lot of reservations about the process, especially from some of the senior members, then this process is not going to work as smoothly as you would like. Make sure that you have all of the buy-in that you need from those in charge before you even begin.

*A*nother thing that you may notice as we go along here is that the Lean method is one that a lot of variety of businesses can use and see benefits. No matter what kind of business you are trying to run at the time, go ahead and take a look at Lean and what it can do for you. There are no limits and you will be thankful that you tried it out. This is not something that works for everyone, such as some small businesses that may not be able to take on some of the costs, but it can show improvements for everyone.

**Important Lean Principles**

From here, we need to take a look at some of the important principles that come with Lean. These will ensure that we are able to work with the Lean methodology and that we are able to get the most out of this in the process as well. While the whole idea of

Lean was originally developed in order to help out the production and manufacturing industries, it has actually been so good at its job and so effective that many other industries and businesses have been able to take it on and adapt it to work with some of their processes as well.

*W*e can all agree that every business wants a chance to increase their profits, to reduce the amount of waste that they have, to make sure that their customers are getting the best experience possible, and they want to be able to do all of this as efficiently as possible. This is where the Lean methodology can take a step up and make all of this happen.

*O*ne thing that we need to consider before we try to adopt the processes that come with Lean though is that there are a few tenants that come into play here. First one is that when we make some of these changes, we need to make the incremental changes, rather than some big ones all at once, and then the second tenant that we have to work with is that the company must have a high level of respect for their employees and the customers. If these are not in place, then Lean is not going to work out all that well for your company.

*S*o, let's look into these a bit more. The first tenant that we talked about is how a business needs to focus on some incremental improvements. These improvements are usually small things that we can do to make the business better. They do not have to be done overnight either. The business needs to have a plan and needs to keep moving forward all of the time. But they do not have to completely redo everything either. For example, moving where the supplies are kept so they are closer to the work-ers, saving space and the movement that employees do can be something that reduces waste (the waste of time), and can help provide more value to your customers. This is a small change that you can make, but it is often enough to make some big differences.

*Y*ou should take a look at all of the processes that are going on with your business and then determine which changes you can make with them. And then one by one, go through and make some of these changes and see what a difference it is going to make. Some of the smallest things that you do for your business in terms of change will make the biggest difference and can make you and your employees that much more efficient overall.

*A*ll of these can lead to more waste in your business, and it is important to avoid them as much as possible. When you take a step back and look objectively at the system you have in place, you are likely to see several spots where you are able to make improvements. Even if these are small, or incremental, changes, you will be amazed at what they can do to eliminate waste, speed up your process, and even help customers enjoy a better experience.

*B*ut when working on the Lean methodology, we can't forget that there needs to be a high level of respect for people. This tenant is meant to apply not only to your customers, but also to your own people, the employees. When we show respect to the customers, it means that we go the extra mile any time there is a problem. We listen to them and then work to make the experience better. We help to fix the problem, and maybe even throw in something extra to help it get solved.

This same idea needs to be applied to your employees when you are working in the Lean process. When a company wants to respect their team, they will work on creating a strong internal culture that is dedicated to teamwork and treating the employees fairly. Employees will learn that they are valued, and their opinion means something, and that they aren't just another number that brings in the money. Any business that wants to implement the Lean process will need to improve employee morale, teamwork and more because they realize that by improving the team, they are able to effectively improve the company as well.

## Lean to Give You the Edge

Before many modern businesses entered the digital age, it was easier to see what kind of margin they had with sales by taking on all of the costs that were the most relevant at the time, and then adding on a reasonable amount for the profits of the company to get the margin and then call it all good. However, there are a lot more factors that we need to hold onto now and consider when coming up with this profit margin, and because people are able to shop from anywhere they would like around the world those margins are getting smaller and smaller.

In the past, you would go to your local store and get all of the items that you need. There wasn't really that much competition that wasn't just a few minutes away. Then the advent of the digital world and lots of screens all around us made it easier for consumers to go out and find many of the items that they wanted without having to stay in their locality. No longer are we stuck with just going to the store that is nearby, we can get things shipped to us from all around the world if we want.

*W*hat this is going to mean for lots of businesses is that they have more competition. They are not able to just go against some of the similar and smaller companies that are in the nearby area, but they have to compete with others like them all around the world. Since it is easy for customers to go online and compare prices and quality before shopping, it is harder to really get a say in how much you can charge for a product because you have to keep it comparable. If you don't, then no one is going to shop with you any longer.

*B*ecause of this, there are not as many options available for companies when it is time to make some real profit margins, which is why it is harder now than ever for companies to make it in the world of business. We have to make sure that we really know the industry and all that comes with it, and that we can reduce the unnecessary parts of our processes ahead of time, or we will never make enough money.

*T*here are many companies who will choose to figure out what their profit margins should be y looking at what the customers are the most likely to pay for some of the products and goods, and then they will take the journey backwards from there to see whether this is something that they can manage. The ideal world would have it where we are able to reduce the first price, the price that customers are likely to spend, by at least five percent to add in some more competition for yourself, while still providing some good customer service. This may not be a very large amount to work with, but it can bring in some more customers.

*W*e have to remember here that no matter what your company specializes in, you are going to find that there are a few Lean principles that we can add in and see some results that will help us out This is going to help us to improve the amount of value that we can provide to our customers, and during this, we can still find ways to show those customers that we appreciate their business. As we go through more of this guidebook, you will see some more of the ways that we can do this and how simple it can be.

*O*ften we are able to manage all of this by taking some time to really listen to our customers, and learning what their needs and wants are all about. Value is going to be generated when you can add something new, something that is tangible and something that will help to improve or modify the most common aspect of a good or service that is being provided. The goal that we are able to get with this is to make an improvement that the customer appreciates enough to actually purchase, so when they get that benefit for free, they will see this as a viable and good reason for your service to cost a bit more in the beginning.

*A*s a business owner, you will find that the added value that you want to use should be something that the customer can claim as possible. If you do not do this well, then the customer will feel like they were misled, which is going to harm your business overall. Making the value that you add in something that is easy to show off or see, or something that is actually a really huge value is so important during this step.

*A*nother thing that we need to consider here is how to reduce our costs as well. every business has to be able to keep their costs down as low as possible. If they don't, then it is hard to gain some of the competitive advantage that we want along the way. This cost reduction is going to make sure that we can stay as competitive in our industry and our market as possible, will make it easier to put our products at a good price point, and can bring in some more money in the process.

*T*o make sure that your company is able to reduce the costs that they are dealing with on a regular basis, we need to be able to reduce the waste that happens, which is a big thing that we will discuss more about as we go through Lean Six Sigma. Here are three types of waste that we need to focus on and all of them can be helpful to your process and for making a good income.

*T*he first type of waste is known as Muri. This is the waste that will show up any time we have too much variation in the processes that we use the most. Then the second type of waste is known as Muda, which is going to be the seven main types of wastes that we will talk about below. And we can then end with the third type of waste, which is known as Mura, which will be any of the waste that we deal with and that happens due to some fluctuations in demand.

. . .

*M*uda is going to be the waste type that is seen as the easiest for us to control and we can eliminate it fairly well in the process. There are seven wastes that fit in with this one as well and knowing what they are all about can make a big difference in the amount of success that you are able to see with your own business. The seven main types of waste that we are able to focus on when we talk about Muda, and that you should spend your time learning more about and eliminating along the way include:

1. **Transportation waste:** This is going to form when information, materials, and parts for a task aren't available because the processes for allocating these resources aren't working the way that they should.

1. **Waiting waste**: This can be created when there is some part of the production chain that has time periods where they aren't working on a task. This could happen because they don't have the right parts or they are waiting for another group to finish first.

1. **Overproduction waste:** This can occur when the demand is exceeding the supply, and the business doesn't have a good plan in place to help deal with this. The Lean system is designed to make sure that this ends up at a zero to help the supply and demand for a product to be in balance.

1. **Defective waste:** This is another part to watch out for. This type of waste is going to appear when a part of your operating process starts to generate some issue that must be sorted out later on, often when the product is in the hands of the customer.

1. **Inventory waste**: This is often going to appear if the production chain ends up remaining idle between runs. This can happen because that part of the chain doesn't have all of the physical materials that are needed to run all the time.

1. **Movement waste:** This can occur when information, materials, and parts must be moved around in order to complete that part of the process.

1. **Additional processing waste**: This can be generated if the work completed doesn't end up adding any kind of value for the company.

*I*n some cases, we are able to add in something that is known as an eighth form of waste in some circles. This is going to be the waste that we will see when some of our team is not utilized to their full potential along the way. This is more common than it may think and it will include times when someone on our team is put into a position where they are not allowed to use all of their skills and their potential. There is so much that your company could unlock if you used this more, and that is a big waste of their talents and a big waste for you. This is also a waste type that would talk about when some of the people on your team have to spend time working on some tasks that they are not really trained to spend their time on.

## Creating a Lean System

As we go through all of this, you may be a bit worried about how we are supposed to make all of this come together. We will walk through a few of the chapters in this guidebook about the actual steps that you can do and all of the great aspects of creating this system, but we are going to look at a bit of it here to see what this is about and to show you more how easy this can be.

To make sure that your business is able to create its own Lean system and then implement it, and to ensure that this is a system that will last, the first thing that we need to work on is considering the absolute easiest and simplest means that you would have at your disposal in order to get your product out to the public, and then see if you can actually make that happen. From that point, you need to be constantly monitoring the processes that are in place to make sure that we are able to support the business because this helps us to get some breakthroughs in performance from time to time, which are always great for our business.

. . .

*W*hen we are done with this, we are able to move on o some of the final steps, which allow us to implement some of these improvements when they do come along. While there are a ton of tools and theories that we are able to use to make these steps happen, the fact that all of this is creating the Lean system, and it really isn't as scary as you thought, can show us that Lean, even though really effective and great to use, is not as scary as you thought.

*W*hen it is time to create our own Lean system for our business, there are a number of parts that need to come together, and we need to keep them in line. We first have to keep in mind that while profits are nice and keep the business running, they are not everything. There is a lot more to running your business than just making a ton of money. When you work with the Lean system, the end goal here is to figure out whether it is possible to make some improvements to how efficient you are, and if you can cut out a few parts of the process, while still providing some good quality to your customer.

*T*he good news is that if you use the Lean methodology well, you will be able to go through and see some more profits than you did in the past. But if you go into this only worried about making a ton of profits, then you will miss out. You will start cutting things left and right, and that may make you more money for the short-term. But when the customers start to get those products and try to use them, they are not going to be all that happy with the quality and they won't come back.

· · ·

*T*he better option to work on here is instead of having all the focus on the money, you can focus more on streamlining your process and getting it to work better as much as possible. You may have to come up with some costs upfront to deal with this. While it seems like you should be saving money here instead of spending, it is going to be fine. Rest assured that all of this is going to come back in higher profits, thanks to the improved efficiency it provides, at a later time.

*O*f course, there are going to be some limits that occur with this, and there are times when the gains aren't necessarily going to be worth the amount that you spend on them. To figure out where this line is, you can use a value curve that shows you how any changes are going to affect, either positively or negatively, your bottom line. companies often work with this value curve when they would like to compare several services or products based on the data they have and many other relevant factors. This can help make decision making much easier to handle.

*T*he next thing to concentrate on is treating tools as what they are. While there are countless companies who switch over to a Lean style of doing things, they may find that it is an easy trap to slip Into when they take the available tools to the extreme, even to the point of following them with a near-religious fervor. It is important to keep in mind that the Lean principles, while very helpful and can do a lot of things for your business, are just guidelines and any of the tools that you choose to use are just added bonuses to help your company complete its work as efficiently as possible.

. . .

*T*his means that if you need to use these tools to get more out of the process and to provide some added benefit to your customers, then go ahead and do it. But it is also important to know the limits of the tools, and their purpose, and then use them in the proper manner.

*T*he final thing that we need to take a look at here to make sure that we use Lean well is that we have to be fully prepared to follow through on our system. Lean isn't something that will work well if we just take a look at it and then pick and choose the parts that seem good or seem the easiest for us to work with. And you will not see results if you go and give it a try for a few weeks and ten abandon it along the way. even if you bring on a good professional who knows how to do Six Sigma or Lean at the beginning of the whole process, it is still going to go over to your team leader at some point. And if you are not prepared to use this for the long haul, and you are not properly trained, this can be an issue.

*L*ean and Six Sigma, especially when they are combined together to make something new, can do some wonders for your business and can really help to reduce the waste that you have taken on. It is never a bad thing to work with lean Six Sigma because you will love the results. Just be prepared to take a good hard look at your own business and your own processes, realize that you need to have everyone in the company on board, and know that this is a process that once you start, you will have to stick with for a long time to see the best results, and you will soon start to see the benefits of Lean Six Sigma.

# WHAT IS SIX SIGMA?

WE TOOK some time to talk about what the Lean method was in the past chapter. There are so many benefits to using this and getting the most out of this system that it is no wonder that so many companies want to take the principles that come with it and put them to goo use. But something that can make your business even better is when we combine Lean with some of the processes of Six Sigma as well. This can take your business to the next level and give you some of the best results that you have been looking for.

*N*ow that we know a little bit more about the Lean part of the equation, it is time for us to move on and look a bit more at six sigma. If you have been going through and learning how to run your own business for a number of years, it is likely that you have heard about Six Sigma and what it is about at some point. This is known as a method to improve quality that is used to help a business owner find the defects that show up in the business model. We are then able to reduce these defects and make our company more effective than it was in the past.

There are a number of methods that can do the same kind of thing, but Six Sigma is the most effective to help get this done. This method is also a good way to minimize all of the defects that may be present in the service or a product that a business has to offer. With Six Sigma, all the errors that are committed are costing the company either in losing customers, having to replace a part, waste of time or material, redoing a task at least ne time, or missing some kind of efficiency. In the end, this costs the business and Six Sigma is able to come in and reduce these losses to help the business to grow.

This was a methodology created by Motorola in the 1980s, so it has been around for some time and has ben able to prove itself. The company, during that time, was working to find a way that they can take their defects and measure them at a granular level compared to some of the previous methods they had used. The goal with all of this was to find a way to reduce these defects to provide their customers with the best product possible.

What happened in all of this was a huge increase I the levels of quality that they could provide in their products, and it wasn't long until the Motorola company was able to get the first Malcolm Baldrige National Quality Award. It didn't take much longer when that was done before Motorola was showing off Six Sigma as a method and soon there were a lot of other companies who used this and took on the rewards that came with it as well. and you will be able to take some of the parts that come with this and utilize it to help your company to grow and save money.

## Why Use Six Sigma?

While we are here, we need to take some time and learn why it is so beneficial to work with Six Sigma, and what this methodology is really able to bring to the table in terms of the work that we can do. There are a lot of reasons out there why a business would want to implement and work with Six Sigma, but some of the main ones that most companies will talk about when it comes to this include:

1. You will find that the quality of a product that you can provide to your customers will improve by leaps and bounds when you use Six Sigma. The same can be said when we look closer at some of the productivity of the company.

1. The number of defects that are possible with this that happen out of a million opportunities will go down quite a bit. This means that if the quality of the product is able to improve way more than a company can do on its own, then Six Sigma is successful. And the fewer defects that you get in a product, the happier the customer will be.

1. The result of any process that is defined using this method

is going to be based on the data that was collected and looked through, rather than the company relying on some of the assumptions that people in management are trying to make. This ensures that your decisions are backed up and secure, rather than letting you fail.

1. The amount of profit that your company will receive will grow quite a bit. This means that the company now will have growth in terms of more profits and more opportunities that they are able to work with.

1. This methodology is able to call on a business to come up with a more integrated and correlated approach to help them to solve all of the problems that are already found in their business.

1. Some of the other cost-cutting measures that companies will use are not always the best for each company. Six Sigma will prefer in most cases to get rid of all the costs that are not adding some good value to their customers.

1. The net costs of production that you will get when you are creating and manufacturing a new product will go down, which can save you a lot more money in the process.

1. When you are able to reduce how many defects you are dealing with, a company is sometimes able to look to the future and raise some of the expectations that they have.

1. It is also possible to work with Six Sigma in order to meet some of the needs and expectations of more of their customers. This is because the company is able to use this method to provide them with the product they already know ad love, but the customer can come in with higher expectations that it will be good, that it will last a lot longer, and that the product will do what the company promises.

1. The internal understanding that shows up inside a business through the various departments can actually go up with this method. This means that all of those who work in the business will really know more about the inner workings of each department and how a problem is really solved.

1. When a company uses Six Sigma there seems to be more happiness and job satisfaction from the employees. Because of the increase in job satisfaction, the amount of internal communication that is going to happen inside all of the company will go up as well.

1. The amount of time that is spent on production while manufacturing one of the new products that you want will decrease. This will allow a business to come in and deliver that service faster than ever before.


1. The market value of that company is able to really go up and see some big increases because of all the other factors that we have been able to discuss here.


*A*s we can see, there are a lot of really great benefits that come with using Six Sigma and making it work for our needs. It is really a tool that a lot of businesses are able to use so that they can earn more money while providing their customers with a really high-quality product in the process.

*W*hile there are quite a few reasons why customers and businesses love working with this method, we need to remember that there are some people who are not that fond of working with it and may advise against it. We are all for Six Sigma and what it has to offer, but it is still a good idea to know some of the drawbacks and some of the things that we need to watch out for along the way.

·  ·  ·

*T*o start, Six Sigma has set up a standard 3.4 defects per million opportunities. For a lot of companies, this is going to sound like a great number and will make it better for them to provide the highest quality of products and services to the customers who use them. However, this is not always the optimal number to go with depending on the process that you want to work with. You may do something that has to do with the well-being of a person. That would maybe push the standard of quality up a little bit higher.

*I*n addition to this, there are some companies that are going to work just fine if they have a lower Sigma level than that. Many find that there really isn't a clear justification as to why they would want to be that high and they could choose the level that works a bit better for their own needs.

*D*PMO

One thing that we need to work with is known as DPMO. You will find that when we talk about Six Sigma, the term defect is going to show up on a regular basis. The goal of a company that is using this is to learn how to reduce how many defects show up, which can help them to reduce waste, provide a better product to their customer, and save more money so they can make that money as well. but that brings us to the point of what a defect is all about.

. . .

*T*he term defect is going to be seen in this method as any nonconformity that shows up in the output that is lower than anything that the customer sees as satisfactory. The number of DPMO, or defects present per million opportunities, is going to be something that we can use in order to figure out which part of the scale on Six Sigma that process is corresponding to.

*Y*ou will find that many companies throughout the world are going to be somewhere between three and four on this scale. This doesn't always seem like a bad thing, but it really implies that they are losing about a quarter of the revenue they should be making because of these defects. Clearing up at least a few is going to make a world of difference and can help your business to survive in the real world.

*T*his is where Six Sigma is able to come into play. It is going to help businesses out and provides them with some of the methods that they need in order to move up to the next level of Sigma and can reduce all the waste and the defects that show up. This will then be an effective method that will help you to earn ore in profits.

## *D*MAIC

Another thing that to consider here is DMAIC. This is going to be used to help us look at the process that we are already using and can make it easy to modify it this ensures that our processes are more compliant with the methodology and that they are more efficient. Some of the parts that we need to remember about the DMAIC part here includes:

1. **Define:** This is the part where the company will need to define all of the goals for the improvement of processes. This needs to be done in a way that they are matching up with the strategies of the business and some of the customer demand as well. you will not really get that far in your process without first defining some of the goals that you want to reach and which processes need to be improved the most to reach these goals.

1. **Measure:** This is going to help us to see the current performance of the systems that your business has in place right now. It is going to take some time here to gather all of the relevant data and can be used later in the process. Measuring the data that you receive is going to be important and we must ensure that we are working on the right tools to make this happen.

1. **Analyze:** This is the spot where your business will analyze the current setting and then observe how this relationship between the key parameters and the performance work. Lean analytics can be a good tool to use to analyze this situation and make sure that the improvements are working the way that you want. If changes need to be made, then this analysis will showcase when this needs to happen.

1. **Improve:** From the other steps, you should have a good plan to know how to improve the process you are doing here. This will ensure that you can optimize the process and earn as much money as possible for the business.

1. **Control:** Here we are going to need to control the parameters before they can really effect the outcome.

## *D*efining

*T*his is a really important part of the process that we need to spend some of our time on. It will ensure that you are able to work through the whole idea of Six Sigma and can make it easier to handle along the way. This does not have to be a complicated process and the DMAIC acronym will make it so much easier for you to keep going and to implement Six Sigma into your own business as you go along.

*A*gain this starts out with the step of Defining. If you don't know what your problem is and how to work with it, you have nothing to work with in Six Sigma. You have to come up with some really clear ideas of the goals of the project and both the deliverables of the customer, both the external and the internal ones, will be defined. The more details that you can add to this, the better it can be for everyone because it puts us all on the same page to start with.

This is the piece that will help us focus the most on some of the projects that have the highest impact, and can help us to learn which metrics out of all the choices that will make sure we see success. You can consider who your customers are and what kinds of requirements they have for this product. You can consider what these customers have for expectations. And you can go through and define the boundaries of the project, including the points to start and the ones to stop. You can work on the process flow and map it all out.

**Measure**

When we are all done with the defining stage, it is time for us to move on to the measuring stage. This is going to be the part where we will document the current process, the forms of measurement that we want to use will be validated, and then the performance that we use as a baseline will be assessed. This will take some time to work on and we need to really be careful about the measurements that we need to work with.

You can view this as a similar method as using the surveys you send to customers to determine a short-fall. This step will help you to collect data from a lot of sources so that you can then use this to help you figure out what types of defects and metrics that you want to use to help with measuring all of it.

. . .

*T*here are a number of tools that you are able to use during this phase and some of them will include the measurement of process capability, some basic Pareto charts if you would like, the Gage R & R, process flowcharts and even some trend charts. Use as much information as you can to help you measure the results that you have and to make sure you really know what is happening as you go through this process.

**Analyze**

*W*hen we are done with the defining and the measuring phases that we talked about above, it is time for you to work on the analyzing phase of all this and figuring out how everything is going. This is the phase that will ask us to focus on isolating some of the top causes that will be there for our Critical to quality characteristic, or our CTQ. This is whatever metric we are using as part of our measuring through this process.

*T*he ideal here is that we do not want to have more than three causes that we want to control in order to see this successful. If there are more than this, then the scope we work with is too broad and we need to make some changes to ensure that this works the way that we want. Having more than three means that your team did not take the time to really isolate the most critical causes or that the goal of any project you picked was just too ambitious. Try to scale it back down to three or less to make this work a bit better.

. . .

*T*his is also the step that we will use to identify any gaps that show p between the current performance that we have and the goal performance. We can also use this as a way to prioritize some of the opportunities for improvement that we want to meet, and to find out if there are some root causes to any variation that we want to work with.

*A*s with the other options, there are a few tools that we are able to work with to make this analyze stage as successful as possible. You may find that working with the time series plots, hypothesis testing, scatter diagrams, fishbone diagrams and more can provide us with some of the data that we are looking for. You need to figure out which one will work the best for you based on the data you have and what you would like to accomplish here.

*I*mprove

*I*t is now time for us to move on to the fourth step of this process, one that allows us to take all of the data that we got from the other stages and put the together to see whether we are able to make some important changes and see some improvements that will benefit us in so many ways. This is going to focus on the idea that we must have a full understanding of the main causes, the same ones that we were able to find in the analyze step that we did.

· · ·

*T*he intent of doing this phase is to either be able to control or eliminate these causes so that we can get the performance that we want in the process. This is also where we can ask our tea to work with technology and discipline to see some good results. And with both of these, the team will come up with some creative and innovative solutions that can prevent problems and fix them when needed. An implementation plan is also going to be developed and then used when we are in this stage.

*T*his is the stage where we will find a lot of really neat tools that we are able to work with. Some of the tools that you may want to use to make this one work include the regression analysis, the Design of Experiments and even hypothesis testing. This will depend on what your goals are all about and what you hope to do along the way with this stage.

**Control**

*A*nd finally, we are able to move on to the final step of this whole process. This one will take a bit of work, but will ensure that the project we take on will work and can provide us with some great options to see continuous improvement. This is a stage where we will take all of the improvements and then work to control them. The reason that we want to control this is to make sure that we get some lasting results and changes that will stick around for a long time to come.

. . .

*T*he best controls that you can come up with will be the ones that don't require a lot of monitoring; it is preferable if you can go with some that don't need any monitoring at all. This can include things like process design or some product changes that you are not able to reverse. But we can also work with other options like the procedures we see with setup, process setting, and other improvements that will necessitate us for monitoring and more.

*T*here should be steps taken through all of this that will ensure our process is not going to revert back to some of the old ways of doing things. When there aren't some immediate changes that show up, sometimes it is easier to go back to the way that things were in the past. This may seem like the easier way to get things done. In reality, it is just going to make things a whole lot harder and will make us miss out on some of the neat things that we can do with Six Sigma.

*W*hen we use all of these steps together in the full implementation of Six Sigma, the steps that we just talked about with this process will help to turn your business around and can make all of the difference in the amount of success you will have. Make sure to add them to some of the processes that you accomplish, and you are sure to see some amazing results in the process.

*D*FSS

The option above is just one of the ways that you can

work Six Sigma into your business. Now we need to divide this up a bit more and see what else is possible here. A business is also able to go through and design a brand new process, doing so from scratch, and still work with this kind of methodology. This would be done with something known as DFSS. When a new process is started this way, then DFSS is going to be the one that we can use. It is similar to what we talked about before but since we are not working with a process that is already in existence, we are going to switch it up a bit.

The DFSS that we are talking about here is going to require that we work with an approach that is known as IDOV and this stands for:

1. **Identify:** This is where we will identify and then define the goals of the process. These need to be consistent with the standards that are found in our industry and the demands that come with the customer.

1. **Design:** This includes taking into consideration all of the solutions that are possible and then picking out the one that is the most optimal for what we are trying to do.

1. **Optimize:** This is when we want to optimize the performance of the application. You are able to work with different methods to make this happen such as advanced simulations and some statistical modeling as well.

1. **Validate:** This is when you are able to verify a solution that you chose and check to see whether it is actually working and doing what we ask

*N*ow, there will be some situations where the DMAIC that we had in the last section can be changed and will turn into the DFSS. This happens when we look at the processes that we use and find that they don't work well for our needs or they are irrelevant. You can decide to redesign them here and get the best results in the process.

*T*he DMAIC process that we talked about before is known because it can help to eliminate some of the problems that result in variabilities in manufacturing and some of the other processes that you want to work in your business. There will be some situations though, when there are no improvements that you can make that will actually help to change the processes that you already have and you need to make some big changes to see some good results.

*W*hen this is something that happens in your business, it is required for you to put a new process in place, then you will want to try something new in the process. And one of the options that you have available for this one is known as Design for Six Sigma, or the DFSS that we were talking about above.

. . .

*T*hough DFSS doesn't actually come in and design a new part or process because each company will have to tailor their own design process specifically to its own products or services, it can make processes more robust, less wasteful and less costly. While DMAIC is the find and fix methodology that you can use, DFSS can be defined as more of a preventative and proactive method that you can work with. It has an ability to help us predict more abut the potential issues that will save you company time, prototypes and validation tests, and that can give you a launch that is less expensive in the long-run.

*T*here are a few key aspects that we need to consider when it is time to work with Six Sigma, and learning how to do each of them will make a world of difference in the success that you see. Some of these you should consider includes:

**Understand your own customers**

*O*ne of the very first things that you need to plan out with DFSS is to compare the requirements of the customers with your process capability. To do this, DFSS users have to understand the expectations of the customers when it comes to the product or service that you provide and then you can identify which will be the focus of your efforts with DFSS. This will involve listening to the voice of the customer, and not your own voice, prioritizing the response of he customer, and then finding a target and range that you can measure out for these requirements.

. . .

*O*nce you have a good understanding of these expectations, then it is time for you to make sure that you understand more about the capabilities of these processes. And to do this one, we need to answer a key question for all of our processes:

"*H*ow often will this process cause us to fail to meet the requirements of the customer?"

*W*hen you can compare the customer requirements and the capability of the process, you will then be able to predict the level at which you can meet the expectations of the customers. If this level is not high enough for your needs, then it is time to make some changes.

**Prediction equations**

*A*nother principle that is key to working with DFSS is to understand more about the relationship that happens between the outputs and the inputs, which we can all the prediction equation. This equation is something that we can determine with the help of many methods. You can figure it out by getting the data from product drawings and a process map. You can use principles that work with the chemistry, geometry, or physics of the design that you are working with. Or you can work with the Design of Experiments to help you to see what is happening between the outputs and the inputs as well.

. . .

*N*o matter which method you use to figure out the prediction equation, knowing it will allow you a good way to make predictions on whether the current, or the planned design, will be able to meet the expectations of the customer. And if it doesn't meet those expectations, you should take a look to see what needs to be changed on it.

*P*rediction equations are so important because they allow us a way to create some robust design, which means that they can be used to fully understand what effect each of the chosen inputs will have on the output. Tis makes it a lot easier to make some adjustments to the design until you hit the right target. From there, you are able to choose some of the settings that will reduce your variability.

### Determining what equals success

*T*he final thing that we need to work with is how we will determine whether we are successful or not. There are a few critical factors that will help you to determine whether implementing DFSS was successful or not. The first factor that you should consider is the stability in the critical processes. Prediction is at the very heart of DFSS, and prediction will rely more on understanding the process capability.

*T*he second part of this that comes into play is making sure that we can find some cross-functionality in the process. This means that the stability that we can get with the stability has to be able to interact with the requirements of the customer, which should then be communicated back in terms that are measurable and quantitative.

*A*nd then the final part of this that we should take a look at is that we need to implement the DFSS into an environment where there are some clear targets set for the quality, the performance, cost, and delivery. There needs to be some good rewards for your design team, ones that are based on the achievement that is measured at the end of it all. This helps to keep people motivated and will make it easier for everyone to come together and see some good results with the process.

*T*o make sure that any implementations that you do with DFSS are successful your design team needs to start focusing on just one single pilot project so that they can get a good handle on the tools and the disciplines that are involved. And, just like all of the other endeavors that we do with Six Sigma, it is also a good idea that your teams work with a practitioner who is experienced and knowledgeable and who will guide them in all of the steps along the way.

*A*s you can see here, there are some really neat things that we are able to do when we take the Six Sigma methodology and try to add it into our own business. It is simple to work with and allows us to find out where some of the defects in our business are, and how we can fix them up for our needs as well. We are going to look more in depth about how this process works and how we can ensure that it does what we want to make our business better, to make the customer happier, and to bring in more profits overall.

# ARE THERE DIFFERENT LEVELS TO IMPLEMENTING SIX SIGMA?

WITH THAT INTRODUCTION to Six Sigma, it is time for us to move on a bit and look at some of the levels that we need to follow in order to actually implement Six Sigma and see some good results. The role that someone is able to play when they implement Six Sigma often depends on the amount of training that they have, and the experience they have when it comes to Six Sigma, the position they have in the company, and more.

## The Roles of Six Sigma

The design that comes with Six Sigma is that there has to be some professional quality management roles for everyone who is part of the team. They have also come with a ranking system that is similar to what we find in martial arts so that we can know who within the business who is working with Six Sigma. Some of the rankings that come with this method includes:

· · ·

$\mathcal{T}$he executive leadership. This is going to be anyone who is considered in the top level of management of the business and may include the CEO as well. these are the visionaries that are able to authorize the others on the team and can provide them with all of the resources that are needed to improve a process. You need to make sure that those in the leadership include some of those who are in the higher levels of the company for this to work. Without some of these people as support, it is impossible to get Six Sigma and all of the processes that come with it to work well.

$\mathcal{T}$hen we have the Quality Leaders or the Champions. These are the individuals who will be in charge of implementing and integrating the methodology throughout all of the company. These individuals will be the ones chosen out of upper management and they will be mentors to the Black Belts to keep things running smoothly.

$\mathcal{T}$hen we have the Master Black Belts. These are those that the Champions are able to identify and they will be the experts who do the coaching in Si Sigma. They will be kind of the guides to the Black Belts and some of the Green Belts and they can assist with the Champions when it is necessary in implementing some of the Six Sigma processes through the company.

$\mathcal{T}$he next level is the Black Belts. These individuals are going to work under the help and the guidance of those Master Black Belts that we talked about above. The main goal of these individuals is to make sure that they supply the ideas that

41

come with Six Sigma to any of the projects they are working on. It is also possible that they will be the ones in charge of executing this kind of project. They will need some direction from the levels ahead of them but they must have some of the right leadership qualities to help them perform their jobs and get it all done right.

*W*e can then move onto the Green Belts. This group is going to move us out of some of the leadership roles a bit but they will still have an important role to getting things done. These individuals will be responsible for implementing Six Sigma inside the business process. It is possible that at times they will work with some of the other projects that the business needs. The belts that are going to be above these will devote all of their time and energy to Six Sigma, but these individuals may be working on some Six Sigma processes while handling other projects that the business needs to function and keep going.

*T*hen we can end with the Yellow Belts here. These are going to be the employees who have had some training with the techniques that are necessary with Six Sigma, but they do not really have a chance here to take that knowledge much yet and apply it to a project that is relying on or using Six Sigma. This gives them a lot of potential to work on tis and see some great results in the process as well.

*E*ven though each level is going to handle the projects in different ways, all of these will be important when we want to implement Six Sigma in our business. This is not a process or a method where eon or two people in the business can do the work and it will still be effective. In fact, this is an extensive process that is often going to need most of the people inside the company working on it at a time, or it will not be successful at all.

*H*owever, it does take some work from the top management, and others who know more about Six Sigma and how it works, to make sure that your business can really make this work well for them. Everyone can come in and play a role in Six Sigma, which is why it is so important for a company to implement it throughout their whole business, rather than in just some small parts of it, and why it is so important to make sure that everyone is allowed to work on it as well.

## *I*mplementing Six Sigma

You will not start out one of these Lean Six Sigma programs by launching right into as many projects as you can. Instead, you will need to spend your time following five main stages that will help you make this a reality. Six Sigma is a strong methodology that will help your business to move deliberately to success, but you have to follow the right steps to make it a reality. The five major stages that we are able to see with Six Sigma include:

1. You will initialize the whole process by establishing some of your own goals and then installing the infrastructure that you would like.

1. You will then deploy that chosen initiative by assigning,

training, and then equipping your staff to make this happen.

2. You can then implement the projects that you need so that you can see an improvement in the performance that you work with, which can then yield some of the financial results that you want.

1. You will then work to expand out the scope of your initiative to include some of he additional units of organization that you really need in this process.

1. It is then time to sustain the initiative. You can do this with any of the realignment that you need, the retraining, and some of the evolution that shows up during this whole process.

*T*he initiatives that you work on with Six Sigma are really just programs. This means that you have to take the preparation and planning that you would with a program to make this work, starting out with a prescriptive set of readiness tasks along the way. the first stage, which is all about initialization, will include selecting out the core team that you would like to work on the project, preparing some of the infrastructure that is necessary to make this happen, and then enabling some of the processes that you need to do.

. . .

*A*s a part of this whole process, the executive training will take time to prepare the senior leaders and all of the executive team. They will all get a good overview of some of the deployment processes of Six Sigma and what they can expect out of this whole thing. The executive is then going to agree on all of the macro items that need to be done, including the time frames, the scope, the goals, and some of the objectives. During this one, the team will need to issue a commitment statement that is formal and make sure that the constituents and the employees all see this as well.

*T*hen it is time to move onto the deployment stage of this one. This is all about setting the infrastructure in motion to start with. With a supporting infrastructure, the goals of the company and the metrics have to be established, then we can work with our deployment stage. This begins when we pick out the champions and the first candidates that work as yellow belts, green belts, and black belts.

*T*he Champions in this will be fully trained in all of the methodology of six sigma, the principles of working and implementing this method, and some of the other stuff that they need. This provides them with the right background to work on the project and they can lead the rest of the business through with the first Six Sigma project in no time.

*T*he core team that has been chosen will go through and deploy the infrastructure based on what was determined in the first step. According to the plan for deployment, the first waves of belts will be trained and then given their assignment for what projects to work with. All types of belt training will include defining, characterizing, and improving a work process as part of the training that will happen.

*T*his is a process that will extend out the time that it takes to train the employees, the trainees who go through it are able to deliver some results to the bottom line as they work on completing some of the initial training that they would like to do. It ensures that everyone has a chance to work on a project and see some good results, even though it can slow down some of it.

*T*hen we move on to the implementing part of the process. When the belt training is done on the first wave, some of the early success that is seen here is all about creating momentum and you should see that the initiative is going to gather some more traction. As the successes continue on, you will find that the initiative is more infectious and you may be able to turn around some of the skeptics who work with you as well.

*D*uring your implementation stage, which is where we are now, the practitioners will spend some of their time defining and mapping out the processes, finding some of the most important indicators, collecting data on performance, and then characterizing some of the process performance they need to work on. They will also conduct some statistical analysis, discovering the root causes that come with the problem at hand and work to improve the amount of performance they can see.

. . .

*T*his is an important part of the process because it means that when you reach it, your company has worked to root out waste, increase the amount of productivity that they have, lower the costs, and decrease the cycle time. This is a good sign that Six Sigma is actually doing the work that it promises.

*W*hen you are done implementing and seeing how great this whole process can be, it is then time to move on and take a look at how you can expand it out to other parts of your company. A six sigma project is often done on just one smaller part of the business, though the other parts are aware of it and actively supporting it. This way, if something doesn't work, we can really catch it and make some changes before it gets too hard to handle or before we waste a lot of time and money implementing the wrong solution to the whole business.

*O*nce we have implemented the process and we know that it will work, it is time to take that idea and expand it out to all parts of the business, at least the ones that are relevant to that solution. Following some of the first waves of success that you see with implementing all of this, the company will then need to expand Six Sigma to some new locations, functional areas, and lines of business.

*T*aking the time to introduce some of this six sigma to the different lines of your business is going to be its own initiative and will include some of the previous stages as well to make it work for you. Don't think that this is something that must occur overnight. It is a process and can take some time and energy to accomplish. The good news though is that some of the lessons you learned from that first deployment will be shown in the revisions to the implementation plans in the future.

*W*hen we are done with all of that, it is time to work on sustaining this and turning your business into something of a self-healing culture. This initiative, when it is all done, will change the character of your business. The Champion and the leader of deployment will then shift over to sustaining direction away from a project orientation into a process management kind of approach. This means that the tools we use in Six Sigma will move to more of a supporting role as part of how the business and work processes execute most efficiently and effectively. The tools will start to enter in as the toolbox of the company though they will be used in different ways now.

*I*n this new phase, which is known as the sustain phase, the culture is more about self-healing. This project is going to be your new tool to help you address any of the issues that occur in the future, thanks to some of the new initiatives and outside forces that may show up.

*T*he training that will happen with Six Sigma through this will support some of the needs of the projects and it can be integrated in with the other methods to support any of the processes that you work on. Training will be used more as a refresher for the existing staff when it is needed, and it is a good way to enable some of the new acquisitions, hires, and contractors to get p to speed on this kind of culture when it is necessary.

# WHAT TOOLS CAN WE USE?

THE NEAT THING about working with Six Sigma is that there really are a ton of tools that we are able to use in order to get the amazing results that we want. These are going to be important tools to work with because they ensure that we provide some good management to the business, and they can be used in a successful manner even if you are not working with Six Sigma directly. Some of the tools that work well with this kind of methodology, and that you should take the time to explore and see how they work for you include:

## The 5 Why's

First on our list is known as the 5 Why's technique. This is one where we want to explore some of the causes and effects of a problem that we want to solve. The goal that we get with this one is to find out the root cause of the problem and not just the one that first appears. Each of answers that we are able to get with this will dive us a bit further down and can help us to really figure out what we need to fix and work on to see results. The name comes from the fact that we are meant to ask Why 5 times, as a minimum, to make sure that we can solve the problem.

*K*eep in mind when you do this that not all of the problems that you work on will come with one root cause. If you would like to be able to go through and figure out more than one root cause, then we would just go through and repeat this method, asking a different sequence of questions this time and each time that you use it.

*I*n addition to all this, this method is not going to come with some hard and fast rules that you need to follow. It is more about exploring what is going on with some of the work that you do and seeing if you can get under the surface, to figure out what is really wrong with something, and then make it better from there. An example of following this option would be the following:

*W*e are working with a problem that says our car is not working. Some of the why's that we would ask here include:

1. Why? Because the battery is not working.
2. Why? Because the alternator is not performing well.
3. Why? The belt that is on our alternator has broken in half.
4. Why? The belt is something that I or the previous owner should have gone through and fixed a long time ago, but did not.

5. Why? The maintenance schedule on the vehicle was not followed.

*T*his is just one example of how we are going to work with this method to ensure that we get the best results. This one helped us to see that there was an issue with the vehicle. You can definitely go through and do more than five of these if the problem needs it, but your goal is to get at least five so you can go through all this and figure out what is really happening.

## *A*xiomatic Design

Another option that we can use is known as the axiomatic design. This is going to be a method that we can work with that helps s to analyze some of the transformation of needs of a customer into the design parameters that we need, the functional requirements, and the variables of the process. This method gets its name because it is going to work with the design principles that will govern the process of analyzing and making decisions. The two axioms that we are able to work with here include:

1. **Axiom 1:** This is going to be the independent axiom. It is there to make sure that we are able to maintain some of the independence of the functional requirements that we use.

1. **Axiom 2:** This is going to be the information axiom. This

will be there to help us minimize the informative content of the design that we work with.

## The Cost to Benefit Analysis

NO matter what kind of business we are in, we need to be able to do an analysis to see if the cost to the benefit will make sense for what we want to do. This is known as the CBA approach and it is meant to help us to estimate the weakness or the strength of a lot of alternatives at once. We are able to use it with transactions, project investments, and other options if we would like. And it is a good way to figure out which option, out of several, is going to be the best. The two main purposes that come with this include:

1. To determine whether a decision or an investment is actually a good option for a business. This means that we need to have all of the costs be lower than the benefits. You may also want to spend some time to see how much this is. If the benefits are not higher than the costs, then it is best to walk away and try something else.

1. Then we also have to be able to use it to find a good way to compare the projects that we want to work on. This can involve comparing the total amount that you think each of these options is going to give you, or the benefits that you expect to see out of each one.

The benefits, and then the costs as well, will be shown in terms of money, which will ensure that it works the best for the Six Sigma option. In addition, you are able to adjust them into all of this to make sure that they count the time value of money. This is a good thing because it makes sure that all the flows of costs and those from benefits over time are able to be shown in a common bias as we go along.

There are a few steps that we are able to follow in order to use the CBA tool for our own benefit. Some of these steps will include:

1. We first need to be able to define the goals and then the objectives of an activity or a project we are working with.
2. We can then go through and list out the alternative projects or programs that we could put in there as well.
3. List out all of the stakeholders who will want to be kept up to date with this one.
4. When we get to this part, we will go through and select all of the measurements that we would like to use to make sure that all of the elements are measured out when we work with the costs and the benefits.
5. You can also spend some time here predicting the outcome that we will get out of a benefit and the cost that we will get when using each alternative over a certain time period.
6. It is also possible to convert all of the costs and the benefits so that they are in the same currency if necessary to make sure that he comparisons are a bit easier to work with.

7. Make sure that as you go through this, you apply the discount rate if there is one.

8. Then we need to go through and calculate out the net present value of the project options that you want to consider.

9. When all of this is in line, we need to do something known as a sensitivity analysis. This is going to be a study of how the uncertainty of the output, using a mathematical system, can be shared to different sources of uncertainty in the inputs that you provide.

10. After all of this is in place you can then look it over and determine which option is the best one for your needs.

## The Root Cause Analysis

This one will often go by the name of RCA, and it is the method ha we want to use when it is time to solve problems. Often it will have a focus on finding the root causes of a problem. A factor is going to be considered as his root cause if you are able o take it out of the equation and then that problem does not show up again. To keep it simple, there are four main principles that are found in this method and they include:

1. The RCA has to be able to describe and define the problem or the event properly.

2. It needs to be able to establish a good timeline from the normal situation until the crisis or the final failure happened.

3. It needs to be able to distinguish between the root causes and the causal factor.

4. Once it is implemented, and the execution is constant, the RCA will be moved into a method of problem prediction as much as possible.

*T*he main use that we are able to get with RCA is to use it to make sure that we can identify and then correct the root cause of an event, rather than just trying to hide the symptoms. An example of this is if a student is in school and then gets a really bad grade on one of there tests. After looking into it really quick, it was found that those who took the test near the end of the day got worse scores than the others.

*T*hen with a bit more investigation, it was found out that these students had less ability to continue their focus and pay attention to the test that was in front of them and this lack of focus came from them being hungry. So after being able to look at the root cause here and finding out that it was all about hunger, the testing time was moved to right after lunch to avoid this problem and the students were able to do better on the test.

*N*otice with this one that the root causes are going to show up in many levels, and that the level for the root is going to be where the current investigator decides to leave it at for the time. Even with this, this is still a good way that we are able to figure out why one process in the business is not behaving in the way that we want and then we can go through the right steps to find a good solution to fix that problem.

. . .

## S IPOC Analysis

As we can already see here, there are a lot of analysis that we are able to work with when it comes to Six sigma, and we are going to spend some time on another one here. This is a tool that we can use to summarize some of the inputs that we get and then the outputs of at least one process. And then all of this will come out to us in the form of a table. The acronym for this kind of analysis is suppliers, inputs, process, outputs, and customers and these will be the columns that show up on your table.

S ometimes this is turned around so that the customers are put in first, but it will really be used in the same way no matter how you treat this. SIPOC is presented at the beginning of your efforts to improve the process, or you can use it during the define phase of DMAIC that we talked about before. You will run across three typical uses of this depending on how you would like to use it and these include:

1. To help out those who are not really familiar with using a particular process.
2. To help those who maybe have a little familiarity with that process, but who may be out of date with some of the updates and changes that have come with this process. Or maybe these individuals haven't been able to use it in a long time so they need some help getting updated.
3. To help those who are out there and trying to define a new process that we are able to use.

# Value Stream Mapping

This is a fun one to work with and you will most definitely bring it out at some point if you plan to work with Six Sigma. When it is time to work with value stream mapping, we are working with a method that is there to analyze the current state of a business and then can help us to design a new state to use sometime in the future. It is meant to take a product or a service that your company already offers from the very beginning and then gets you to the end point where that product or service is given to the customer. The hope with this one is that the process is able to reduce wastes, especially compared back to the processes that the company is using right now.

To value stream means that we need to learn how to focus on each and every area of the business that will add in some value to a product or a service. This allows us to figure out where the wastes are going in so hat we can remove it if possible, or at least reduce it to make things work the way that we want. This can help to increase some of the efficiency of a business and is a great way to improve the productivity as well.

There are a few different parts that we are able to work with but the most important is to figure out where some of the wastes are coming with this business. Some of the most common types of waste that we can find in Lean include:

1. **Faster pace than necessary:** This is where a company is going to try and produce too much of the service at once.

This is going to end up damaging some of the production flow, the quality that is found in the product, and the productivity of the workers.

1. **Waiting:** This is he time when goods are not having someone work on them, or when they are not being transported to another part.

1. **Conveyance:** This is the process that we will use to move the products around. It can look a things like moving around too much, too much area between certain parts, too much back and forth to get it done, and more.

1. **Excess stock:** This is where the company has too much inventory sitting around that is not being used. This can add on to the costs of storage and it is a lot harder to find some of the necessary problems if we are not paying attention to this at all.
2. **Unnecessary motion:** this is waste that has the employees using more energy than they should to pick up and move items.

1. **Correction of mistakes:** The cost that the business will have when they try to correct the defect they work on.

*T*his is a method that we will see often when we talk about a Lean environment because it helps us to go through and look at some of the design flows for all the different parts of the company. This is often something that is tied in with manufacturing, but you can find this method in lots of other industries including software development, product development, and even in healthcare in some instances.

As we can see here, there are a lot of parts that come with working in Lean Six Sigma, and all of these tools can help us to learn more about our business and about the things that are slowing us down and making it really hard for us to see some of the results that we want. Depending on the process that you would like to improve in your own business, and some of your own goals, you may want to pick one of the methods over the others. But all of them can provide you with some of the information and the understanding that you need to see some great results.

# THE STEPS OF LEAN SIX SIGMA

NOW IT IS time for us to get into some of the fun stuff that we can do when it is time to work with lean Six Sigma. While some companies decide to start right from the beginning with a new process to get things going with the hopes that this will make it easier to get fewer defects and to help them provide better customer service, this is not always necessary. It is likely that you have some kind of process in place for your business and with a few simple changes, you are able to take your process and make it so much better, without having to throw the whole thing out the window. This is why it is common for companies who want to work with Six Sigma to just work with the DMAIC method to help.

We are going to take some time to look at the various steps that we are able to utilize in order to accomplish something with Lean Six Sigma, and dive into some of the steps that you need to take to make sure that you get the best results. This will make sure that you can cut out the waste, improve the process that is already there for your business, and serve your customers better than ever before. When it is time to work through some of these steps, you can use the following to help:

*D*efine

This is the first step that we need to take some time on. This one requires that we take a look at the data or the process and then find out if there are some areas or a certain process that can be improved. This will be the nature of the problem that we work with. During this step, you will need to form a team and help them train in how to use this method, which will make it better to have someone to work on these improvements with you. You must work with a team that actually believes in Six Sigma and what it is all about, and one that is motivated or this will not work out well.

*T*hen we need to move on to identifying the people or the customers who would be impacted by this process the most. You can then document some of the critical requirements for these customers and then create a team charter that will detail things like the business case, the scope of the project, the statement about the problem and more. This is going to make sure that you get through the defining steps a little bit easier. You can use some of the tools that we talked about in the last chapter to get this done.

*M*easure

Now it is time for us to take a look at the second step an this one is all about measuring. This one will take us a bit more time to work on and complete compared to the other one.

But when we are in this stage, we need to define the parameters that we plan to use to help us measure whether the performance or the process is actually improving the way that we want it too. You will also have to have a good baseline of the performance and an idea of how well you think this whole thing will be able to improve when you are done. All of these are good to make sure that you have a plan, that you follow the plan, and to make sure that the plan was actually successful when you are all done.

*I*t is possible that during this phase you will need to spend some time looking at and then being able to identify some of the key defects that are found in he process. Then, when you are able to define the ones that you would like to improve, you have to take the time to collect the data to make it easier to analyze the differences that come between the performance that is designed and the current performance that is already in place.

*T*his does sound complicated, and it does need a lot of data and measurements to make sure that it is all going to match up and do what you would like. But it is worth your time to learn how to make this happen and how to do the right measurements. The more accurately you can do your measurements now, the easier it will be to see if things worked out later on.

*A*nalyze

Now we are on to the third step of analyzing. Once we have some measurements and a plan in place, we have to be able to analyze whether things are working out the way that we would like. This phase is where we will take all of that data that we collect ed and used in he first phase and then analyze a bit more what the gap is between the desired and he current performance. We want to also figure out what it would take to bring both of these together to get some amazing results.

When we get this far, we can work on a RCA again to help us figure out what is there and what is causing the gap between the goals that you set earlier and the current performance. This is something that we will be able to calculate in a number of ways but often you will see it done in financial terms because it is easier to handle.

## Improve

The analysis phase is sometimes really short and some-times it will take a bit longer. It all depends on the processes that you are working with and what your overall goals are. It sometimes also depends on the amount of data that you are trying to work with as well. when that is all done, it is time for us to work on the fourth step, which is figuring out what steps we need to take to improve things.

During this step, we will need to take all of the steps that are necessary in order to improve the issues that were found in our product or our processes. Then we are going to device a set of solutions that we are able to use. Sometimes you will be presented with just a handful of options that will work, and then other times there are lots of options and the decision can be a bit harder to work with. From there, whether you get a lot of choices or not, you can then pick out the one that is going to provide you with the most efficiency and the best results overall.

*T*he main outcome that we are hoping for when we use this step is to design a plan for performance improvement. The more information that we are able to add to this, and the more in-depth information that we can add in, the better it will work. The whole point of this plan is that it works to provide us with a measured difference, one that we can even see, in the process that we already have so that we can see in real-time the defects start to decrease.

## *C*ontrol

The final phase that we are able to use when working on Six Sigma is known as the control phase. This is where we are going to come out with some of the plans of project management, and some of the procedures that we need to follow to make sure that we can sustain and use the process that has been created.

*T*his is a really important step that we need to maintain and work with, though there are many companies that will forget all about it. How do we know that this method is going to work if no one will actually follow the plan that you come up with during that time? It is during this phase that we need to document the process that we made revisions to, device, and then deploy the response plan. then it is time to transfer this information about the new process over to those who would use it the most, like the management of different departments.

. . .

*W*hen we are able to take these six steps and combine them together, you can find that there is a lot of efficiency in Six Sigma, and that his method will work great for you. It helps us to figure out where the problem parts of our company are located, and then gives us the right data to actually improve and fix them. It is time consuming and not something that gets done in one afternoon. And you have to make sure that each person who is in your company is on the same page and ready to go with it. But when we can get it all to fit together and work well, it can really help improve our business.

# FIGURING OUT THE SCOPE OF YOUR PROJECT

THE NEXT THING that we need to take some time to work on here is how to figure out the right scope of our project. We already know some of the basics that come with using Six sigma, but then it is time to go through and start out with some of the scope that we want to use with this process, and how we are able to make this work for some of our needs as well. Let's dive into learning a bit more about the scope of any project that is Lean Six Sigma approved and then see what we are able to do with this.

## Scope the Project

So, a project in Six Sigma is going to start out as some kind of practical problem, one that is already adversely affecting the business. Then it is going to end with a practical solution that will ensure that the business is able to improve how well it performs. If you are able to find a project where the business is able to improve a current process, then this is a good candidate to using that as your Six Sigma process.

. . .

*T*he focus of your project with this method is going to be that we want to solve a problem that is already harming some of the key elements of performance for that company. This can include things like the output capacity, the cycle time, the revenue potential, the organizational viability, the employee and the customer satisfaction, the costs, and the process capabilities.

*Y*ou will want to get started on this kind of project by stating out what the problems with the performance are all about. You want to also work with some terms that are easy to look through and that can define some of or expectations. These also have to relate back to the levels of performance and timing that you hope to get when it is all done with.

*A*s you go through and try to define the project that we want to use, you need to be careful about a few things. First you can't work on all projects at the same time as you use more about Six Sigma, it is likely that you will encounter a whole bunch of wastes and things that you can improve. You need to put your focus on just one or two of these at a time, see how they go, and then when they are all done, you can make some changes and work on some of the other options. Some of the other problems that we can consider when we pick out one of the projects that we want to work on includes:

1.  Issues that will have an impact on our Earnings before income tax, or on some of the net profit that we make

before the income tax. You can also look at those that have a lot of value strategically.

2. Issues that are going to give you results that will exceed the effort that is required to get them to work.

3. Ones that are not quick or easy to solve if you use some of your older methods in the past.

4. Issues that are able to improve the KPI, or the key performance indicator by more than 70 percent over the existing levels of performance where they are now.

*I*t is also possible that there is a type of flow that will come into some of the projects that you want to use as well. you will want to maintain this flow in order to make sure that you get the right process down for your project. Some of the projects that we can consider here when we worry about the type of flow that comes to our projects includes:

1. **Practical problem:** This is going to be a chronic or another systemic problem that is going to affect the success of the process that you are in.

1. **The six sigma project:** This is going to be some kind of effort that is defined well and that will state your problem out in terms that we can quantify and that have known expectations.

1. **Statistical problem:** This is the problem that is data-oriented and is going to use facts and data to help figure these things out.

1. **The statistical solution:** This is going to be a solution that is driven by the data and has some confidence and risk levels that are known. This is in comparison to some of the solutions that say "I think" that may have been used by your company in the past.

1. **Control plan:** This is going to be a method that we can use to make sure that our solution to that problem can be used for the long-term. You do not want to come in here with a solution that works now, but then a few months down the line it doesn't work well at all. You should go with a solution that will work for the long-term and can provide you with the great results that you want.

1. **Practical solution:** This is the type of solution that is not seen as irrational, complex, or expensive. The best part of this one is that you can implement it without a ton of waiting or lots of problems along the way.

1. **Results:** These are going to be some of the tangible results that you can get. You can measure it out in a financial

manner or in some other ways that show it is really benefiting some of the companies.

You ou will sometimes find, that even with Six Sigma and all that it can provide to us, that working on a new project is not always as easy as it seems. You want to make sure that you go with a project that is there o help your business out and will be able to help us work with the methodology of Six Sigma to get it all done. When this happens, it will do some amazing things for your overall business that you can't even imagine right now.

## Transform Your Problem

When this is done, it is time for us to take a look at how to transform the problem we want to work with and change it up so we can actually come up with a good solution. The first step that we took a look at above is all about scoping out a good project that will work for your business. When we have had the time to take a process or a problem that we would like to fix in the company and then we frame it to the potential project that we want to use with Six Sigma, it is time for us to put that problem through a few tests to make it go through a change. We want to transform it over to a business problem that is practical over to what we would call a statistical problem.

The he reason that it will change between these problem type is so that you can really identify a statistical solution. This is a lot easier to understand in a few cases, and then you can move that back over to a new practical solution, but only after you receive the data and the information that you need to make this happen. This is why we need to define the project, an when we do, you must make sure that you state it out with statistical language. This ensures that you, and anyone who is working on the same team as you will be able to use the data, and nothing but the data, to solve that problem.

*A*s long as you use the data well, it is not able to lie to you. If you use it wrong or you don't read it the right way, then you will end up in trouble. You can get some really great results from the data that you can make some smart decisions from as you go. Many companies find that changing the problem into some form of data can help them to see just how big the problem is from the start.

*F*or example, maybe you see that your customers are not coming back to you. But when you can change this up and see just how many customers have left your business, or how much this loss of business translates over to a dollar amount, you can see that it is a much bigger problem than we may have thought to get started.

*D*ata is also a good way for you to work with some of the facts that are right there. Too many times your business will rely on intuition and sometimes educated guesses. And some companies have made major decisions based on their gut feelings and hope that this works. This is not a good idea because there is no data out there to see what is going on and to ensure that you make the right decisions. Using data gives you cold hard facts that make sure you pick the right choices that will work for you, and will take all the intuition and guessing out of he mix.

*T*his is also a good option to work with that will show you that just throwing time and money at the problem is not always the best solution for the problem. This seems to be the way that some businesses will choose to handle things, and it is not going to really help you to come up with a good choice at all. It can sometimes cost you a lot of profits ahead of time, and can then make it so that your customer service goes down in no time.

*W*hat we need to work on with this is some practical solutions instead. A project that will rely on Six Sigma is going to make sure you have practical solutions. They will not be that hard for us to implement into the current business model that we want, and it will not require us to have a lot of resources to get the improvements in place. That is one of the best things to consider with Six Sigma because we often go into this methodology assuming that this is going to be hard and complicated to work with, but in reality, this is simple to work with and can provide us with the results that we want without a ton of work.

# WHO IS RESPONSIBLE?

ANOTHER THING that we need to consider when we go through the process of Six Sigma is who will be responsible for all of he different parts that happen in our project. This is a bit harder to do than some other methods because the chain of command will not work the same as they do in your traditional business. But knowing what role all of he people in your business have at different points in the process can make a world of difference.

In addition to some of the other steps that we took some time to work on, we need to spend some time setting up the responsibilities and who gets to handle each of these for all parts of the process. Problems can start out in the functional area and they can change as we go through all of this. But if you go through with this, and you set up the responsibilities the right way, then this process will work out well.

. . .

*T*he responsibilities, accountabilities, and the deliverables of the project will be divided between the managers as well as between the different belts that are part of Six Sigma. This will allow everyone has a job and that there isn't just one person who goes through and provides some input and does some work. You don't want one person doing all of the work through this, and you don't want one person who assigns all the work and then doesn't do anything in the process. A good balance that involves the whole team will be the best options to make this done.

*Y*ou also need to include some of the employees who are not part of management. These individuals are responsible for implement the solution that the whole team agreed on in the beginning and then seeing some of the benefits. We must have all of these parts come together. The managers, and the nonmanagers need to all work together through this methodology to make sure that we will see as much success as possible.

*T*hese relationships will make sure that the deliverables from Six Sigma are not going to get lost or fall through some of the cracks as we work with all of this. The whole point of working on this is that the project has to bas to team effort. Even when we get to the beginning stages of this and you work on the phase of Define, the phase where all of the people have to figure out what project needs to be done first, we must make sure that there are other Six Sigma belts there working on it together.

· · ·

*O*f course, those who are part of the Belts will only take on about 20 percent of the responsibilities when it comes to defining the improvement, and the same is said when we work with managing that improvement as well. then, when it is time to go through and implement these project, we will switch things around and the Belts will be in charge of doing most of he work that is needed in order to fix the problem. This is why we have to work with both parts of this and we can't allow one person to do it all or exclude anyone who is part of the company.

The way that we go through this responsibility is going to really depend on what works the best for your needs and to make sure that the work gets done well. The managers and the owner of the project, or the company, will be able to help set up these responsibilities. But you should consider some of he belts that are present with the employees and always take into consideration the skills and experience that your team has to start with. This will ensure that the job is done as efficiently as possible and can make a world of difference in how valuable your employees feel.

*T*he main thing to consider here is that before the project is started, you need to make sure that everyone who is part of the team has a job that they are trained how to do, and that they all know what their role in the process is. This will make sure that everyone is on the same page and can see some good results in the process.

# HOW TO KNOW WHAT SOLUTION IS THE BEST?

SOMETIMES, you will get started with a project and find that there is more than one solution that can help you to get to the end of the goal. This is sometimes hard to work with because how are you supposed to know which solution is the best one for you to get done. This chapter is going to take a look at how you can pick out the right solution for your needs to ensure that you effectively take care of the problem and see some good results.

One way to make sure that you can actually implement your own six sigma project is to start out with a pilot project. This will help you to figure to figure out what problems are actually there in your own business, and you can then move on to how you can make these work for you. You can also determine who will be responsible for the work, and then get input from a lot of different people through the process. Remember that this whole thing will only work out well if each person in the business can be involved, rather than just one or two people at the top.

· · ·

When we get to this part, we need to know only take a look at the problems that are the big issues for the business and that we need to work on improving, but we have to pick out a solution. When that solution is picked out, you can implement the solution and do some follow up to help ensure that the solution was implemented well and whether it is working or not. We will look at how to go through each of these parts to see how we can handle the solution, and even how to pick a good one.

## How to Pick Out a Solution

At some point in this process you will need to look through the main problems of your business if you are using Six Sigma, and then you need to figure out the best solution based on what problem you face and what resources are available. How you will complete this step will really depend on the problem you choose to fix at this time, but there will be situations where you can pick from more than one available solution from which to choose. So, when we end up with more than one solution to work with, how are we supposed to choose the one that is right out of that?

This is where we will really need to focus on a few of the tools that come with Six Sigma, and then figure out what we can do with each one. This way, you can easily see more about which solutions you can use to make your business more efficient, to reduce waste, and to hopefully ensure that you will make as many profits in the process as possible. This is a tall order for a solution, but it has to meet all of these to make it work. In the end, you should be able to find one solution that is able to handle all of the problems that are in front of you. Do your research

## Implementing a Solution

Now when we get to this part, we have had some time to look at the variety of solutions that are out there and available, and you can choose the one that you think will work the best for this particular problem. When that is done, you need to take that solution and actually implement it. This will be the step where everyone really needs to be on board with one another. If you have troubles with this still, then the process or the solution will not implement well, and the methodology that comes with Six Sigma will end up causing you some failure along the way.

*T*his means that everyone has to be on the same page when it is time to implement this new system. Everyone on the team, no matter what ranking they are or which belt they have in the first place, needs to come together ahead of time and not only figure out the best solution to use for their needs, but also the steps that must be taken to implement this solution as well. this can take some time, but agreement is necessary to make all of this work out.

*Y*ou need all of the people on the same team to come up with the procedures that must be followed to help you implement the right solution as time goes along. This doesn't have to be a complicated process so don't feel like that is the requirement here. You cold simply change up the way that your new employees are trained to make sure they know how to do their jobs. You cold eliminate a few steps out of the process to make it more efficient. You cold even ask those who work directly with the product to clean up their areas or set it up in a new way to make it easier to keep moving and not wasting time.

*A*gain, the steps that you use here will depend quite a bit on the solution that you and the rest of the team come up with. But look closely at the solution that is there, and make some decisions based on what should happen at the different levels of this to ensure you are going to make this work. No matter what solution you go with, you need to implement it in a good and clear way so that all those who have to use that solution understand the new requirements.

## The Follow Up

At this point, we have taken some time go through and figure out what problem we want to work with, and then we came up with a good solution that we thought would be efficient for taking care of the problem at hand. Then we went through and thought of the steps that we needed to use to implement this and to show others on the team how they should get things done. This is a good start to the Six Sigma implementation of a solution. Now we need to take it a bit farther and look at how we can make improvements on the solution as time goes on.

*O*ur hope here is that the solution we chose in the beginning and implemented will actually behave and do what we were expecting. Along with this, we hope that it is a solution that is really easy to implement and something that both the customers and your employees will be fine working with because it doesn't unnecessarily complicate what is going on around them. It will also take away some of the issues that you had before and will ensure that your business can be efficient, cut out some of he waste, and make more in profits all at the same time.

We can't make this an assumption though or we end up missing out on knowing whether the solution is a good one or not. We have to double-check through this that the solution is working for our business, and this means that we need to evaluate it and follow up to see how well it is working. The reason we do this is to make sure that the solution we picked is efficient, that it was implemented well, and that it is actually fixing the problem.

It is really easy to go through and implement a new solution, and then walk away from it, never focusing on what it does in the future at all. Then, along the line we find out that it didn't improve anything or it causes us to lose more money than we were to start with. This can happen and sometimes we will pick out the solution that is not the best option for us. The evaluations and the follow up can make sure this doesn't happen and can alert us to some potential problems long before it happens.

As you get to the point where your project is getting done, it is important to do the evaluation is important because it is going to detail for us what seems to work well and what is causing us some problems with our solution. The workers who help with this can be a really big source of information and you should talk with them to figure out which criteria and evaluation parameters you should go with.

. . .

$\mathcal{I}$t is also a good idea to have a method that is in place to make sure that all of the procedures that were agreed on earlier will be implemented correctly. All managers and those in charge of this procedure should know how to complete these evaluations and how to report them back to you, and even have the right training to fix the behavior if it is needed.

$\mathcal{T}$he point of working with this Six Sigma process is to help get rid of the defects and the waste that show up in your business, while also finding ways to provide better customer service in the process. If you can find a good solution out of all the options that are able to complete these goals, but you don't take the time to follow up with it and ensure that this solution is doing its work, then it was a big waste of effort and time to even come up with it and put it in place. And that is completely against what we are trying to do when it comes to Six Sigma.

$\mathcal{R}$emember through all of this that Six Sigma is a process that actually does take some time and a bit of effort along the way to make it happen. It is not always going to be the smoothest sailing to work with, and sometimes it may cost you a bit of money to start off with. However, if you are truly interested in providing a better experience for your customer, you want to be able to provide some of the best products that you can to the customers, you want to reduce how much overhead is around you, and you want to increase your own profits, then Six Sigma can help you get that done. This chapter took a look at how you can take some of the ideas of Six Sigma and add it into finding a good solution for your business to make you as successful as possible.

# COMMON ISSUES THAT CAN SHOW UP IN LEAN SIX SIGMA

AS YOU CAN IMAGINE, the more time that you spend with Lean Six Sigma, the more you can find some potential issues creeping into the mix. This is not a hard or difficult process to work with, but it is something that takes some time, and a good amount of knowledge, to put in place. If you don't have everyone on the team ready to handle this, or you don't do your follow up when it is time, or someone doesn't understand what they are really doing when they implement this process, all of your hard work can go down the drain.

Six Sigma is not something new in the world of business and many companies out there have given it a try and will talk about how great it can be. Many companies who go through the steps and implement Six Sigma and Lean will talk about how it will improve the processes that they already use, and can make sure they provide the best products and services to their customers. Having the ability to cut down on some of the defects and kick out the waste is the best way to make sure these companies can increase how profitable they are, how productive they are, and how satisfied the customers are with their services.

*H*owever, we have to realize ahead of time that there are some obstacles that will show up when we want to work with Six Sigma and Lean. You have to make sure that you know about these hurdles ahead of time so you can address them before they happen, and so you can get the best results in the process. Some of the most common issues that you should be aware of when it is time to work with Lean Six Sigma, mainly so you can avoid them overall, include:

## *T*he Leadership is not Committed

The first issue is when you have some management or other leader who is not onboard with what Lean Six Sigma is all about. This is not really a method that we can just read about in a book or a magazine once, toss over to the employees, and then just hope that we will see the results and really like it There has to be a good amount of effort from every member of a company in order to make this work and if the management doesn't get along with it, then this will really cause some harm in your success.

*a* true test to see whether a company is really committed to working with this will show up when the management is in charge of picking which employees will go to the project. It is always the best bet to go with those of the top talent, rather than just picking your best friends or whomever seems to be the most available at the time. If the management goes through and randomly chooses people who are available, even though this doesn't make sense and they don't have the right training, then this is starting the whole project off wrong and will lead to some failure.

*I*n addition to this, this is able to reduce how likely it is that the Lean Six Sigma project is going to be a success. This kind of project, in order to see some good results, will need to have some good leaders, those who have dedication to provide the right resources, time, talent, money and more to the Lean Six Sigma project they decide to go with.

*N*ot Understanding the Process

It is really hard to make sure that a methodology is able to work well if you do not fully understand how that methodology will work in the first place. Some companies will choose to grab onto Six Sigma simply because they know other companies who use this or they feel like this is something they should do to get results. Others want to rush into this kind of project because they feel some excitement, but they don't really have a good grasp on all that Six Sigma is about because they didn't take the time to do their research and learn all about it.

*T*he first thing we have to understand here is that it is never a good idea to implement this methodology just because you think it will keep you up with the competition. You should also be careful about not wasting your time is if you think this is a god way to impress those who own a share of your company. If you plan to implement it as a cosmetic change to your business, or you want to implement it without the resources that it needs then this is dooming your project right from the start.

The best way for us to overcome this kind of obstacle is to commit to the process of Lean Six Sigma from the beginning, and give it your all. You can ten make sure that you employ and support the experts in this field on your team before you get too far, easing the process right from the beginning. This is the only way to see success out of this.

Your goal is to get many experts in Six Sigma and Lean to come work for you, or at least train your own employees to become these experts. These experts can work for your company sometimes and other times you may hire from outside areas. But they are there to help make sure you have a focused process, and that you can really pick the ones that will create a big difference in your company. Do not waste your time or the time of your team by using this process only to help with some simple changes that will not really make a big difference at all.

As we have talked about through this guidebook, you will find that Six sigma is able to do a lot of really neat things for your business. With a few changes overall, you will be able to take your company to the next level and really cut out some of the wastes, save some money, make a superior product, and help your customers out as much as possible. To make this work, you must be willing to take on some of he big tasks and you have to understand the process that is in front of you. If you are not willing to work with this process well and you don't fully understand it, then Six Sigma and Lean will not work for you at all.

## You Execute it Poorly

The last issue that we will take some time to explore here is the kind of execution that you would use with Lean Six Sigma. Some people are ready to get on board with this and spend hours learning how to make it happen. They get some training in how to do this and train some of their employees, or hire new employees who know how to do all of this, so that they understand how it works. They pick the right project with the right solution and then work really hard to implement this whole thing. They are the ones who will see some good results.

*A*nd then there are those who may be excited to work with Lean Six Sigma, but they don't have a plan. They may not really understand how this process works but they know that a lot of other companies are working with it and they assume that for them to keep up and see some results, they need to do this as well. They don't train or worry about any of the belts that we will talk about as we go through this guidebook because they don't think it is important. They just pick any old project they want, or one that they have held close for some time, whether it is one that actually fits the mold of Lean Six Sigma and then they wonder why they are ending up in failure.

*I*f you are going to be in the second group, then you may as well walk away right now and not even try to work with this at all. This is really poor execution and it is going to set your program or your project up for failure, no matter how hard you work to prevent it later on. You have to execute the project well and really work well with Lean Six Sigma to see some of the results that you want.

. . .

*E*ven if you have someone with a lot of experience in Lean Six Sigma there to guide you with your process, there will still be certain times when the project will not go the way that you want. And the reason for this is because you didn't execute it properly. This execution is poor and it will cause some problems when your improvements are not aligning with the goals that your company set out in the beginning.

*I*t is also an issue when we find that it reacts and uses that as a way to solve some problems that show up in the business, rather than using it as a way to meet some of the strategic objectives that you have in place. In addition, it could happen when you take a good improvement project that is higher in quality and then you make it focus too much on the outputs that you will get from that project rather than paying the necessary attention to some of the inputs out there.

*W*hen a business is able to use Six Sigma and they understand that these methodologies have to work inside the real world, and not inside of a vacuum, things are going to become so much easier. You need to take some of the method that we talk about here and then make sure that they align up well with some of the goals and objectives of the company. When this happens, then it is easier than ever to stay on your own target.

*I*f you go through this and you work with this methodology, but you still do not see a good gain in productivity, or at least not as much as you had been hoping for, then it is time to do more research and figure out what the reason for this would be. Do not jump to the conclusion that the issue is all about Six Sigma and this methodology that you are using. The reason is that there is something else going on with your business and you need to fix this. It could be something like the project not being managed well or that the leadership isn't taking their own roles seriously in the process.

*Y*ou have to go further into the cause and not blame the methodology. Remember that a lot of other companies have gone through and used this methodology in the past, and seen success. So it is more likely that you are not using this the right way or that there is some other major issue that shows up in your business that you need to fix first to make sure that you get some good results.

*I*f something does show up when you do your work in Six Sigma, a good rule to work with is the 5 Why's. Go through the problem and ask why at least five times. This helps you to get down to the root of the problem. It is possible that the root of the problem is something that completely surprises you, so that can be a good way to really learn what is wrong, rather than making some assumptions as you go along.

*I*f you use the methodology and all of the tools of Lean Six Sigma in the right way, you will really see some amazing results in the process. You may even be amazed at how much time, money, and resources you can save, all while still providing some good services and products to your customers. You can do all of this with Six Sigma, but you will need to be careful and really learn about Six Sigma, to make sure that it works the way that we want it to.

*L*ean Six Sigma is not meant to be a process that is hard to handle, and sometimes it is going to seem like the steps are really too simple to bring on and make much of a difference. There are still some parts in all of this that may cause us some issues down the road. Knowing what these are and how to prevent them will be the best method when you are ready to take your knowledge of Lean Six Sigma and put it to good use with some of your own projects as well. Anyone is able to work with lean Six Sigma and see the benefits, you just need to know how to get this done.

# THE CERTIFICATION LEVELS OF SIX SIGMA

WE HAVE MENTIONED a few times that there are a few certification levels that you can meet when you start wo work on Lean Six Sigma for your own business. These levels will basically tell us how much the individual has worked with Lean Six Sigma and how much they understand about the whole process. You need individuals with all of the various certification levels in place to make sure that Lean Six Sigma is going to behave the way that you want.

For this to work, we must keep in mind that Six Sigma is a methodology of project management that is able to help us improve or profits, make sur that we have a good quality of products, that we can boost the morale of those around the company and to even reduce the defects that we have. Many companies will find that it is useful to helping them reach perfection, or at least as close to this as possible.

. . .

*A*lthough there isn't necessarily a governing body out there that can list out and dictate the rules that come with Six Sigma like other methodologies out there, many companies will offer some types of certification to help individuals showcase how much they know about this method to those who are interested. By becoming certified with Six Sigma you can show others that you are serious about this method and all that it is able to offer. Some of the things that we can consider when it comes to working with the certifications that are available with Lean Six Sigma include:

## *D*etermining the Management Philosophy

The first thing that we need to do here is figure out what our management philosophy and then learn which levels there are when it is time to pick out the right certification. We need to always go with what would work best for the company. So, consider what kinds of management styles would work the best for your company and whether you are already dealing with too much overhead that your business has right now. You can also look to see whether there are some issues with staying consistent with getting things done and consider all of the culture that is out there with your business.

*T*his will really make a difference in what you are able to do with Lean Six Sigma. You have to really know more about your own business and what it has to offer, rather than really working with something that may have worked with another business in the past. You are unique and you must look at some of your own unique situations to make this work.

. . .

*T*he second thing that we need to take a look at here is how we would like to optimize the processes that are already found in our business. Maybe you are a business owner who likes to check on quality and the best way to do this is to make sure that you have lots of processes in place without any variation in them at all. Others are more into going for efficiency or producing a quality product without including as much overhead in the process. When this is considered, it will change the way that you handle your Lean Six Sigma process and what you will do when that is all over.

*T*hen we need to move on and take a look at which kinds of certifications you would like to work on. You can go with either Six Sigma or Lean Six Sigma. These are similar but we do need to consider that there are some differences. The type of management philosophy that you determined before will make a difference in which choice you go with.

1. **Six Sigma:** The first choice that you can make is for Six Sigma. This is going to take the waste and define it as a variation in the processes that your business has. If you believe in having a process that is always consistent, then this is the choice that you would go with.

1. **Lean Six Sigma:** This will be a good combination of Six Sigma and Lean and will provide you with some of its own benefits as time goes on. It is a good method because it will define waste as something that isn't adding any value

to your product or the finished thing that you send out to the customer. If you would like to make sure that you are as efficient as possible, then this is a great level to work with.

## Deciding on the Certification

Now it is time for us to go through on the certification is the best for what your business would like to do. This can take some time, and you have to make sure that you actually have the right employees to make all of this to happen. This will take some time, and is not always as easy as it seems, but we will walk through the process to help you out with this.

First on the list here is to determine what your own role is within the company. This will really help each individual to figure out how high of a certification level they need to get. Think about whether you are a manager or someone who supports the level. Will you be able to make some of the major decisions for the business or just be more of a supporting role? Each person will have a place in this kind of system, but knowing where that place is will make a big difference in the success that you can reach.

Then it is time to consider what kinds of movement you would like to make within the company at some point in your career or what some of your goals are all about. Even if you are not currently in the position of project management, this doesn't mean that you shouldn't do the training and see whether that is a possibility in the future. Always consider what you hope to accomplish in the future and use that to help guide your decision.

*T*hen it is time for us to go through and click out what kind of certification that we would like to work with. There are a number of these, but we will take a look at the top four and see how we are able to make those work for us. These four levels include the yellow belt, the green belt, the black belt, and the master black belt. All of these are so important for making sure that the process will do what we want. Let's divide these up and see what they are about.

*T*here are the yellow belts first. These will be the individuals who have just a bit of understanding of the Six Sigma process. They will hold onto a good supporting roles to help out those who have a higher belt in the process. There are a lot of courses out there that you can pick from because this is a basic option. It at least gets your feet wet in the process and will not make you take too much time. This is a good place to get into things and see what Six Sigma and Lean are all about and you can build up from there.

*W*hen the yellow belts are done, it is time to mov eon to the green belts. These will be those in the company who work quite a bit with the black belts and they are often going to be the ones responsible for collecting up a lot of data. These are the individuals who are happy to work with six Sigma, but who will not put all of their focus on this kind of project. For example, they may work on the Six Sigma project a bit but they will still have some other responsibilities and jobs within the company outside of this. This requires them to have a basic understanding of what goes on, but they can't give their full time and dedication to it.

*T*hen it is time to move on to working with the black belts. These are simply the individuals who will be the managers of any projects that are decided on for Six Sigma. The other individuals of the team, and anyone who is working on Six Sigma and that project, will have to report to these individuals. They will also be the ones wo will come in and dedicate a ton of their time to these projects and they may have very few options or responsibilities outside of this kind of project.

*W*e can finish off with the master black belts. These will be the experts. They have the most training on how to work with Six Sigma, and they are likely to have had some time to work on a project or two of this nature in the past. They will be the ones who the whole team is able to report to if there are some issues or errors with the project, and they will make sure that everyone stays on track with this process as well.

*E*ach of the belts will be a bit different than what we are able to see with this, and it is important to go through and make sure that you have the right people for the job that fit all of these belts. You can provide the right training for your employees to make sure that they are able to handle this and put it together, or you can hire individuals who already have the training. Do not try to take random employees, tell them they are now working on Lean Six Sigma, and then provide them with no training because this will make a world of difference in what you will get out of the process.

## How to Get Certified

Another thing that we need to take a look at when we work through this chapter is how to get the different certifications that are offered here. This is usually not too difficult to work with, though it will take some studying and it does require you to spend your time learning and taking some tests to prove your knowledge. Some experience will be a good thing here as well.

*T*he first option that we can go with when it is time to get certified through all of this is to find a good training program. It is likely that you will have to spend time getting class-room instruction to get this started. This means that you should do some online research to see what options are around you. In some cases, you can do it in your local area and other times you may need to travel. Always make sure that before you go with any program that you get one that has accreditation.

*W*hile the accreditation is important, remember that right now there are not a lot of formal standards that are universally required for these programs so that will make this a bit harder. But there are still a few options of accreditation companies that will verify the data you will learn so take a look at that to pick the right one.

*O*nce you have had a chance to find a program you like, it is time to enroll in that program. You can then attend the right classes and learn all of the material that is required for the belt you want. You have to start out as a yellow belt and then move your way up. So, if you haven't had a chance to work with this at all, and you don't have a belt in the past, then that is where you have to start. Then you can move your way up through the belts from that.

*A*fter taking some classes and doing some of the studying that you should, it is time to take the written test. If you picked out a good test and you paid attention, then this should not be too hard to work with. The written test is all about checking to see whether you are actually learning what is necessary for that belt of Six Sigma. These tests are not things that you can quickly get through and will take at least a few hours so be prepared for that. For example, to get your yellow belt you will need to finish a test that is two hours long, the green belt will put you through a test that is three hours long, and then the black belt will have a test that is four hours long.

*E*ven after going to a class and taking a test, this is not all done. It is now time for us to complete a few projects and see how that can make a difference for us. The final phase of being certified will be the process of doing a few projects with the methodology of Six sigma so that you can really show your skills and what you are able to do with his process. This is kind of like completing a lab to make sure that you can take the knowledge of Six Sigma and implement all that you learned.

*S*ome of the Benefits of Six Sigma Certification

The final thing that we will take a look at here is how we

can benefit when we decide to go through the steps above and get or certification in Lean Six Sigma. The process does take some time, but isn't too difficult, and there are a lot of benefits that you are able to enjoy to make it happen for you.

*H*aving employees who are certified in working on Six Sigma are able to bring in a ton of benefits to your company. You already know how the process is supposed to work and these employees can then be there to ensure that your project runs as smoothly as possible. It doesn't even matter which belt the employee decides to get. All of these are important to helping implement the Six Sigma project and ensuring that we get it done well.

*I*f your current employer is looking to start out with Six Sigma and wants to use this as the method to see some improvements, then it is worth your time to go out and get this kind of certification to make sure you can get promotions and provide more value to your company. This can make it easier for the employer to pick you to work on the project, and it is a fast-track to success in your field.

*T*here may be times though when your current employer is not going to implement Six Sigma at all. This doesn't mean that you should give up and not work with Six Sigma at all. It is still something that can be very much worth your time. You could get it and use that certification later on if your current company decides to go with that method or you can save it and use that as a way to spice up your resume when it is time for a career change.

. . .

*A*nd that is really all there is to the process. The amount of time that is needed to help you complete this kind of certification really does depend on which belt you are the most interested in and how well you can get to some of the training centers in your area. The good news is that with a bit of studying and some time, you will be able to learn all of the necessary steps that you need to take Six Sigma and Lean and implement them well inside of your own business plan.

# TIPS TO MAKE SIX SIGMA WORK
# FOR YOU

BEFORE WE END out with this guidebook, it is time for us to take a look at a few more tips and suggestions that you are able to follow to get the most out of your own Lean Six Sigma process. We took quite a bit of time in this guidebook to learn how this process is meant to work and what we are able to do with it, but there are still a lot of tips and tricks that will make us more successful when we try to implement it.

Six Sigma, especially when we combine it together with Lean, is something that can do a lot for our business. It is a method that is there to reduce most, if not all, of the wastes that or business may produce. When that happens, we can really provide some better products and services to our customers, while increasing the amount of money that we bring in each month. However, there are sometimes when you hear about this option, but you are still a little confused by the steps and what it all entails.

The good news is that there are a lot of tips and tricks that you can follow to make sure that you get the most out of Lean Six Sigma. This is a process that takes some time and resources, and you don't want to waste those hoping that you get it right and finding out in the end that you did something wrong. That is why we will take some time in this chapter to look at the best tips and tricks that you can use to make Lean Six Sigma as safe and effective as possible.

The first step is something that we have talked about a bit before, but we still need to bring it up a bit more to make sure we understand what is going on with this. We must make sure that we have the right amount of commitment from the leadership there to see results. Make sure that everyone at the top of the company is committed to working through all of this. These same people also need to be convinced about all of the benefits of Six Sigma and why they would want to go with this method over some of the other options on the first place.

Along with some of the options that we just talked about, your steering committee needs to be formed right from the start. This is done to ensure that:

1. The goals of the company will still align well with some of the projects that you can do with Six Sigma.
2. The resources that you need to use are all planned out and you already account for the roadblocks and move them out of the way.
3. The one person needs to be there to help lead them all, though they are not allowed to sit there and bark orders out while not helping others during this. You need to pick out a black belt to do this and you should pick out someone who is going to do the best job with all of this.

Along the same lines here, we need to make sure that any of the leaders of our projects are trained well. they need to be the Six Sigma Champions at the minimum, which will be another level above the master black belts and is reserved for the managers who work with this process as well. This is a training session that will take two days and can help the management of your team learn how to lead and run some of their groups in Lean Six Sigma.

There also has to be someone there who will be able to train all of the other belts who will run around your company. And you have to pick the right person who will be able to handle this and do it well. There are a lot of programs out there who will promise that they can do the best job ad will provide you with some good options. But most of them are not that important and not that good, but you can still find some good ones if you do some research. You need to pick out the right person, or the right options, that will make it easier for you to go through and really train all of your employees on how to work with Six Sigma.

While we are going through and picking out the program that we want or employees to work with, we need to check what the return on the training investment should be. If you see a program and it is less than 20 times the training investment for your return, then this is just a waste of your money. Or it is a sign that you are picking the wrong project to spend your time on.

A good way to make sure that you get this new Six Sigma movement going and to ensure that it is successful is to start it down on the shop level, and not just with the management. There are too many times when the management is the ones who get to decide everything. And often this is done without the discussion or input of those who work in the shop. This is really hard and can make people feel like they are not that valuable. How good would you feel if you were just told what to do without any help along the way and without anyone asking your opinion at all?

This is why it is a good idea to get this started right from the shop level. You do not just want to have a few green belts or a few black belts who are doing all of the work during this either. You need to take some time to train the necessary supervisors or operators on the shop floor so that they are able to work with all the techniques that come with Six Sigma. You can use the white belt program to help them get it done without them having to waste a lot of time learning the parts that don't pertain to their jobs.

Doing this is great for your company though because it will help them to feel like they own a bit of the process and like they are able to make some of the improvements as well. you can also reward some of the team members and the leaders who decide to get this certification to help encourage them to see what this is all about and why it is such a good thing to work on.

Along the way, we need to consider a new mentoring process that we are able to work with. This is going to help make sure that anyone who is working on this process, and wants to learn more about it, will have the right guidance to make it all happen. In addition, make sure that there are some options for course corrections on a regular basis and that all of the projects that are decided on and set up will get done on time as we go.

Some companies have found that when they implement the Six Sigma process that having some financial validation to this project will help to increase their chances of success as they go along. There has to be some kind of financial leader in place, someone who is able to sign off on how much the project will cost and how it will come in and save the company some more money. This is something that needs to be implemented during the control phase to make sure that the spending on any project doesn't get out of hand.

A big mistake that some companies are going to make here is tat they will use Six Sigma, but they will classify it in the wrong manner. For example, they may decide to make it the job of the quality manager. The quality manager does come in with a distinct role to get things done, and they are not really there to help manage all of the processes that come with Six Sigma, at least not all on their own. The projects will work so much better when you make sure that you have the right team, and then they have the right training, so that they can handle the project and make it work well.

Create a goal that you share in common with everyone on the team. Once you have decided that it is time to implement the process of Six Sigma, the next thing that you should do is make sure that anyone else who is qualified on your team is aware of the goal and that everyone is on the same page. This common goal is not something that has to be that complicated, but you must show it through an executive directive and you need to make sure that it is a goal that all employees, no matter their levels, have to follow. The pint of this is to reduce some of the variability so that you can reduce your waste.

Part of working with Six Sigma and Lean is that you need to take some time to add standardization into all of this. Any methodology that you implement during this has to include some standardization in order to work. To make sure that you are successful from the start, you must have an approach that is defined and standard as much as possible. If you forget this part, then there are a lot of people who may be on the same team, but they will spend a lot of time redefining it and trying to make some changes.

Standardization is something that seems like it takes out the creativity and some of the fun that can come with a process. That doesn't have to be the truth though. This just sets up some clearly defined labels and ideas of how to get the work done that everyone on the team has to follow to make sure they get some good results in the process. As long as the team stays within those standardizations, you will still be able to encourage you to try something new and be creative.

Remember here that standardization is the process that we need to use in order to allow the people who are on the same team to focus on reducing the standard deviation in the projects that they work with, rather than having to think about how to do the method and pick which one they would like to use to be as efficient as possible. This standardization may take more time in the beginning as everyone is going to learn how to make this work. But as time goes on here, it will make sure that all employees and managers have an approach that is common. And as we learn how to work with this and the steps that we need to take, it can help to reduce the execution time in no time.

In addition, it is going to help create a new language that the whole team is able to work with. It is able to create a language that is common so you can make a good culture of teamwork within that business. This is something that you need to come up with early on in the process, and you need to take the time to train all employees how to work with that method. After some growing pains though, you will find that this is a method that can make life so much easier overall.

Then it is time to map out the plan that you want to work with for Six Sigma. Any plan that you do is focused the whole time and will keep things running on time. To do this, you need to make sure that the plan is mapped out well. you can also make sure that all of the different teams you would like for all of the projects are sorted out and they know what they need to do for each part of the process. And then you can schedule out all of the steps of the process.

While we are working with this, the company has to have a good awareness that the process improvement programs are not going to be implemented within a few days, rather, you will take a few months, and sometimes even a few years, to get all of the processes done and see it all come out. You will see improvements quickly, but the process is something that you want to work on for the long-term as you go through. During all of this, you must make sure that all of your time and money are invested wisely.

Then it is time to move on to when you would like to present your data. This needs to be scheduled ahead of time. Throughout implementing the new program that you set up, you will need to have some frequent reviews and audits. This is done to make sure that you will actually see some good progress that is being made when you do the implementation.

During these scheduled meetings, you would need to present the data, and each of your teams need to describe the milestones that they did, the progress, some of the roadblocks that they encounter, and some of the needs and more that they come across as they go through this. We need to take the time on a regular basis, at least once a month, or more often, to help us to hear what is going on with the process. You can decide how often to do this, but you need to schedule this ahead of time to make sure that everyone is on the same page.

We can ten take a look at some of the methodologies for optimizing any of the non-technical processes that you want to work with. Some of the invisible processes, such as those that are done by your finance team and even your purchasing department. These are important to work with and they have to be defined, measured, and even optimized as much as possible through this. They may seem to be intangible and not directly related to some of the process that you work with, but they are important and you need to consider them and find ways to reduce the waste that you work with in your company.

As we talked about before, you have to make sure that you always pick out the right project. When you handle any of the parts that come with Lean Six Sigma, it is likely that you will take a look at some of the parts that are found in your business and notice that there are more than one project that you are able to handle or choose to work with. This is likely to happen for a lot of companies along the way, so don't be surprised if you can make a list of projects that you need to work on ahead of time.

The problem occurs when you try to take on too much at once. You are not able to handle all of he work that you need at once here. You have to pick one or two projects to work on at a time, and focus your attention on just doing that instead of all of them. You can come back ad focus on more of the options later if you feel that it is important, but you don't have the attention or the resources to make it happen for twenty projects at once.

Do not try to waste your resources or your time on a project that isn't important or will not be able to make a big difference in your business at all. You need to pick out a project that you can work on for a short amount of time and then improve your current processes, while increasing your profits. Make sure that when you get started on this, you will spend some time picking out a project that works well, and training your employees to handle this as well. This will make it easier to work on the project and see some good results.

The final tip that we will take a look at here is that you must pick a good project that will help you to meet all of your goals as a company. As we mentioned, there are always a lot of projects that you can choose from along the way. but if you go ahead and pick out one that doesn't align well with your goals and what you would like to do with your business, then this is not a good project for your business to pick at all. Make sure that you implement a good project that works with your business, or it will cause you to fail, regardless of how much work you spend with that process.

When you take the time to learn more about Six Sigma and Lean and how to make these all come together, you will find that it is a lot easier to reduce some of the inefficiencies that are present and in return for this, it will provide you with some high yields that your company can enjoy for a long time to come.

With this in mind though, you have to check that you invest wisely, that you learn how to work with Six Sigma well, and that you come up with a good plan that works with all of your long-term goals in the process. Being able to do all of this along with Lean Six Sigma is the best way to make sure that you always achieve your financial goals.

# AFTERWORD

Thank you for making it through to the end of *Lean Six Sigma*, let's hope it was informative and able to provide you with all of the tools you need to achieve your goals whatever they may be.

The next step is to take some of the steps and the methods that we have discussed in this guidebook and put them to good use. There are a lot of companies who want to find a way to gain some edge over their competition, who want to be able to provide some better customer service to those who purchase from them, and who want to increase their profits margins. And there are a lot of programs out there that promise to help out with this. But none are as efficient and as easy to work with as Lean Six Sigma.

This guidebook took some time to look more into the process of Lean Six Sigma and all of the steps that you need to take to really make this work for you. No matter what industry you are in or what you sell to your customers, you are sure to benefit from sing Lean Six Sigma to cut out the waste and serve your customers better. The best part is that you can do all of this while increasing your own profits in the process. This guidebook will go through all of the steps to help you know the exact way that you can implement Lean Six Sigma in your life as well.

There are so many benefits to working with Lean Six Sigma, and though there are other methodologies out there that promise to do the same and give you some good results, none will work as well as this one. When you are ready to work with lean Six Sigma and to see what it is able to do for your business, no matter what industry you are in, make sure to check out this guidebook to get started.

Finally, if you found this book useful in any way, a review on Amazon is always appreciated!

Made in the USA
Monee, IL
21 September 2021